Also available at all good book stores

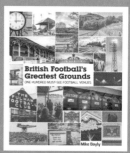

9781785316470

9781785313929

9781785315466

9781785316890

9781785315671

9781785316432

9781785311581

9781848181090

9781908051349

CELTIC
MINUTE
BY MINUTE

CELTIC
MINUTE
BY MINUTE

Covering More Than 500 Goals,
Penalties, Red Cards and
Other Intriguing Facts

DAVID JACKSON

First published by Pitch Publishing, 2021

Pitch Publishing
A2 Yeoman Gate
Yeoman Way
Worthing
Sussex
BN13 3QZ
www.pitchpublishing.co.uk
info@pitchpublishing.co.uk

ISBN978 1 78531 828 3

Typesetting and origination by Pitch Publishing
Printed and bound in India by Replika Press Pvt. Ltd.

Contents

This book is dedicated to Jock Stein and the Lisbon Lions who will be forever remembered and cherished by Celtic fans around the world.

Acknowledgements

Celtic Minute by Minute was a hard but hugely enjoyable book to research, but thanks to certain resource outlets, it was made a lot easier.

The goal times are taken from various sources, but BBC Scotland match reports, Sky Sports games, endless YouTube highlights (and countless newspaper clippings and old match reports that sometimes tested my eyesight to the limit), plus Celtic FC's official website and various other fan sites and stats platforms, such as Opta, Soccerbase, Transfermarkt and 11v11, all proved helpful.

But one website in particular proved a genuine lifesaver. The Celtic Wiki proved absolutely invaluable for the finer points a book like this requires, plus intricate details and exhaustive stats of anything and everything to do with the Celts that helped me put flesh on the bones of some goals (especially those from way back when – in short, before TV), as well as discovering many fascinating facts and insights. An education, in fact.

Also, the Celtic Wiki has many videos and news clippings that make this a site that every Celtic fan should visit on a regular basis. It is a bible for all things green and white and I'd like to send a massive thanks to the dedicated folk who so lovingly tend that site. They do so for the benefit of others and deserve all the plaudits that come their way. Thanks guys – I don't think I could have written this book without your website (www.thecelticwiki.com). And we'll be sending you a couple of copies, of course!

Fitbastats.com is another very useful resource for anybody researching the history of the Hoops – again, these individuals perform a fantastic service with little or no reward.

I'd also like to thank former Celtic striker Georgios Samaras for very kindly providing the foreword for this book. Georgios spent seven very happy years at Celtic Park and was only too happy to help out. As the dreary November weather continued in late 2020, he spoke of his love for the Bhoys as he sat having a cocktail by his swimming pool in Crete!

I'll make a confession, now – one, I'm from south of the border, and two, I'm not a lifelong Celt. I hope that doesn't put you off because since I was a kid, I have loved Celtic fans. That might sound odd, but the sheer size of Celtic is staggering and I've always been fascinated by the vast numbers that watch this grand old football club. I had to look twice at Hampden Park crowds of 130,000+ and the 80,000+ that regularly watched games at Celtic Park over the years. More than anything, the celebrations after some of the goals – the passion and joy – not to mention the noise. That, for me, is what being a supporter is all about. So, forgive me for not being one of your vast number, but it is a genuine privilege to write about your club and I just hope you think I've done a decent job.

Finally, I'd like to thank Paul and Jane Camillin – the tireless siblings who mastermind Pitch Publishing – for green-lighting this series. Having a *Celtic Minute by Minute* was a no-brainer and, we have an end result ...

Foreword by Georgios Samaras

Though I hadn't wanted to leave Manchester City, it seemed that a new manager and a new board were introduced every season during my stay and it was getting difficult to find my best form. I was comfortable in Manchester and I believed in myself, but I remember Sven-Göran Eriksson coming to me and telling me he had a team for me and the CEO approached me and told me I needed to go to this club and talk to them – that's when he told me it was Celtic.

I decided to go and see how things felt but told Celtic I wasn't promising anything – I said I would have a chat face to face and then make my decision. So, I drove to Glasgow and arrived at the ground. After meeting the club representatives, I was shown out into Celtic Park and once I saw the stands and the pitch, I decided that was the place for me.

I knew that I would win trophies, play in the Champions League and achieve the things I wanted to achieve with Celtic, and everything I'd worked towards in my career would be possible. Players need rewards for hard work – not monetary – but medals and trophies, so when your career ends, you have something to show for your efforts.

I joined in late January 2008 on a six-month loan with Gordon Strachan the manager. I came on against Kilmarnock as a sub and scored in a 5-1 win. The strange thing about that game was after the match, Gordon Strachan came up to me and said, 'George, you made a big mess, what are you doing?' I asked him what he meant and he said that the boots I'd scored in were orange and I was like, 'And?' Then he explained a bit more! I said, 'And you're telling me this now? I wore those boots all week in training.'

But he was just joking and I never had a problem about it – but I made sure I wore black boots in our next game!

It wasn't all plain sailing to begin with and Strachan was replaced by Tony Mowbray, who stayed less than a year. It wasn't until Neil Lennon took over that things really started to happen for me. We had a communication problem at the beginning where I couldn't understand him and he couldn't understand me, so we sat down and discussed a way forward and it was good for him and good for me – after that, things went really well.

I was 29 when I left Celtic and I had been at the club seven years. We had been talking about a new three-year deal because I had in my mind that I wanted to stay ten years, but it didn't work out and I moved on. I'd made 249 appearances, scored 74 goals and won seven trophies in seven years, so it was all good.

It's a pleasure to be able to open this book with my memories of playing for this incredible club and, of course, the title of *Celtic Minute by Minute* demands that I recall some of my favourite goals and the minutes they were scored in.

So, where to begin?

I'll start with a goal I scored against Shakhter Karagandy of Kazakhstan in the Champions League in the third qualifying round. We'd lost the first leg 2-0 and we needed to win by three goals to progress to the group stage. Celtic Park was full and we'd gone ahead through Kris Commons in first-half added time, and I scored the goal that levelled the aggregate on 49 minutes James Forrest settled the game in injury time to give us a 3-0 win and take us through to the next phase. It was an important goal and a great turnaround, so that sticks in my mind.

My next memory is my first goal against Rangers. To score a goal in an Old Firm clash and at Ibrox was very special, but on this day in 2011, I was lucky enough to score twice as we beat Rangers 2-0. The first was on 62 minutes and the second was from the penalty spot on 70 minutes – a very happy memory!

Next up, a couple of last-minute winners against Russian sides to send us through to the Champions League group stage. The first was a minute into added time against Dynamo Moscow where we had to overturn a 1-0 first-leg loss. I came off the bench to score our second and give us a 2-0 win and send us through.

Three years later, my last-minute header against Spartak gave us a 3-2 win in Moscow – what are the odds of getting two last-minute winners in the same stadium? That's why they have stuck in my mind!

The last goal I'm going to include was probably not the most important goal I ever scored in my career, but it meant a lot to me and it was a goal I celebrated the most. We were at home to Aberdeen and had gone ahead through Kris Commons in the first minute – but Aberdeen fought back to lead 3-1. We'd fought back to 3-3 and I'd come on as a sub, when the ball fell to me in the six-yard box and I sent it into the net with an overhead kick. I tore my shirt off and waved it around my head as I ran off to celebrate with the fans and it was such a wonderful feeling. That, for the record, was 90+4 minutes!

It didn't mean we won anything and it was just another three points for a team who were already way out in front in the Scottish Premier League title race, but it was just the sheer joy of the moment and the spirit we had shown to win the game.

So, some special goals and the minutes they were scored in, but in truth, every goal I scored for Celtic was special because I loved every minute of my time with the club – and I hope you love recalling some of Celtic's most memorable goals in the pages that follow ...

Georgios Samaras, Crete, December 2020

Introduction

Glasgow Celtic Football Club have an extraordinary history and *Celtic Minute by Minute* takes you through the Bhoys' matchday history and records the historic goals, incidents, memorable moments and the minutes they happened in.

From Celtic's early beginnings and successes to the days of domestic domination; from the great Jock Stein era, the Billy McNeill days, right through to the more recent past and the teams of Martin O'Neill, Brendan Rodgers, Neil Lennon and many others.

Learn about the club's most historic moments or simply relive some truly unforgettable moments from Old Firm clashes past and present, title-winning goals or moments that are simply unforgettable for no particular reason (if that makes sense!).

Included are all the Scottish Cup final successes and goalscorers – that's 40 trophy lifts and counting in Scotland's premier cup competition – plus all 19 Scottish League Cup final triumphs, along with each and every goal the Hoops scored in those finals, as well as – of course – all the goals the Lisbon Lions scored along the way to European Cup glory in 1967. In short, the moments that really mattered and, given there have been more than 100 trophies won by Celtic, a heck of a lot of research by yours truly.

You will also discover just how many times a crucial goal has been scored at the same minute so often over the years. From goals scored in the opening few seconds to the last-gasp extra-time winners, the drama of numerous penalty shoot-outs – and even a coin toss – that have thrilled generations of fans at Celtic Park and around the world. Included are countless goals from Jinky Johnstone, Bobby Lennox, Stevie Chalmers, Dixie Deans, Kenny Dalglish, Charlie Nicholas, Henrik Larsson, Paul McStay, James Forrest, Moussa Dembélé, and a cast of hundreds from the magnificent players who have graced this fantastic club, as well as many players who may not have hit the heights, but still have played their part in Celtic's history.

Now you can discover just when those historic, brilliant or occasionally seemingly run-of-the-mill goals were scored and how they were created.

Enjoy, relive and recall ...

Celtic Minute by Minute

The referee blows his whistle,

and off we go ...

One minute or less ...

6 seconds

16 December 1950

Though the timekeepers and ways of gauging when goals were scored were undoubtedly slightly less reliable than in today's digital world, John McPhail holds the record of scoring Celtic's fastest goal of all time. A couple of passes are made from kick-off before McPhail shoots home with reporters claiming there had only been six seconds played of the game. Even if it were a second or so more, it's almost certainly the quickest the Hoops have ever got off the mark and McPhail would go on to complete a hat-trick in a comfortable 6-2 win at Parkhead – the Bhoys' biggest win since the end of World War II.

12 seconds

16 March 2013

With many supporters not even in their seats yet, Kris Commons puts Celtic ahead with the first attack of the game. Aberdeen don't even get a touch as the Bhoys kick off, pass the ball around before a pass to Anthony Stokes sees the striker lay it to his left for Commons to drill home a dramatic opener at Celtic Park. It is also the fastest SPL goal ever up to that point.

18 seconds

21 October 1970

Willie Wallace gets Celtic off to the perfect start in the European Cup first-leg tie against Irish side Waterford. Played at Dublin's Lansdowne Road to meet the incredible demand, the Celts score almost from the kick-off, with Bobby Lennox racing down the left flank before sending in a low cross that Wallace side-foots home to give Jock Stein's men an early advantage.

40 seconds

1 April 1970

Dubbed the 'Battle of Britain', Celtic were paired with the great Leeds United of the era in the European Cup semi-finals, with the first leg played at Elland Road. The Celts took around 10,000 fans south, looking to see off their English opponents on their way to reaching a second European Cup final in the space of four years – but Don Revie's Leeds, champions of England and with a fearsome reputation for winning no matter what, were strong favourites to progress. But few could have predicted such a dramatic start to the game. Paul Madeley misjudging a high ball and the home defence making a hash of clearing the danger, the ball falls to George Connolly who hits a low shot that deflects off a defender and wrong-foots Leeds keeper Gary Sprake to send the travelling fans behind the goal wild. It was the first goal Leeds had conceded in the competition and also Celtic's first away goal – all with just 40 seconds on the clock!

52 seconds

27 August 2000

Celtic get off to a dream start against Rangers in the Old Firm clash at Parkhead. The Celts had had to live in the shadow of Rangers' domination of the 1990s but will unleash a decade of frustration in 90 explosive minutes. Lubo Moravčík's corner is only half-cleared by the Rangers defence and Henrik Larsson's low shot is swept into the net by Chris Sutton from a yard or so out to put the Hoops 1-0 up.

2

25 October 1969

Celtic secure a second Scottish League Cup in the space of six months with the winning goal coming just two minutes in against St Johnstone. Having won the delayed 1968 final the previous April, Celtic went looking for a fifth successive League Cup success at Hampden Park. With the majority of the 73,067 crowd willing them on, the Bhoys get the early breakthrough that will prove to be the only goal of the game as John Hughes finds Harry Hood in the box, but his header crashes against the bar and Bertie Auld is on hand to prod home the ball from close range. Though there are 88 minutes still to play, the Saints can't find an equaliser and Jock Stein's imperious side claim a 13th trophy in five years.

12 November 1969

In the European Cup second round first leg against Portuguese giants Benfica, Celtic get off to the perfect start. Awarded a free kick 20 yards from goal, Bertie Auld looks set to take the set piece, but had Benfica done their homework, they might suspect that Tommy Gemmell lurking just behind Auld might be the most likely to shoot – and that's what happens, as Auld lays the ball back into Gemmell's path and the brilliant left-back thumps a cracking shot that is in the back of the net before the keeper even sees it, much to the delight of the near 80,000 Parkhead crowd.

6 May 1972

After Jimmy Johnstone draws a foul on the left, the free kick is lofted towards the back post where skipper Billy McNeill finishes with a low shot from close range to put Celtic 1-0 up in the Scottish Cup Final at Hampden Park. It's a terrific start for the Bhoys who will go on to enjoy a record-breaking afternoon against Hibs.

13 March 2003

With just 100 seconds on the clock, Celtic get off to the perfect start in the so-called 'Battle of Britain' against Liverpool in the UEFA Cup quarter-final first leg at Parkhead. With the game hyped up by the media, there is a carnival atmosphere by kick-off and that seems to transmit down to the players, as John Hartson's deep cross finds Alan Thompson who drives the ball back low and hard across the box where Henrik Larsson is on hand to poke the ball over the line from close range – his 25th European goal for the Celts – to make it 1-0.

19 May 2019

On a day of celebration at Parkhead, the Celts take the lead thanks to the talented Mikey Johnston. With the Scottish Premiership trophy lift to come, Neil Lennon's men take the initiative from the kick-off as Ewan Henderson plays in 20-year-old Johnston, and the youngster beats Hearts keeper Bobby Zlámal on his near post to make it 1-0.

6 February 2021

Stephen Welsh puts Celtic ahead in the first attack of any note against Motherwell. The 21-year-old defender rises highest from a corner to claim his first senior goal for the Hoops to put Neil Lennon's side 1-0 up at Celtic Park.

3

26 April 1969

A day Rangers fans want to forget in a hurry as Celtic tear into their fierce rivals from the kick-off in the Scottish Cup Final at Hampden Park. Celtic, backed by 60,000 fans in the tinderbox atmosphere, take the lead when a looping Billy McNeill header from a corner finds the top right of the Rangers net to make it 1-0.

9 May 1998

Knowing victory will give Wim Jansen's Celtic a first SPL title since 1988 and deny Rangers ten championships in a row, the Bhoys get the early goal the sell-out Parkhead crowd demand against St Johnstone. The opening goal settles the nerves as Paul Lambert sets away Henrik Larsson who cuts in from the left and then fires a shot into the top-right corner for his 19th of the season.

18 February 2006

Mark Wilson creates the opening goal of eight as Celtic destroy Dunfermline Athletic on their own soil. Wilson skips past a challenge on the left of the box before firing a low cross into the six-yard box for Stiliyan Petrov to fire home and make it 1-0.

1 December 2013

Kris Commons gets Celtic off to the perfect start at Tynecastle in the Scottish Cup fourth-round tie at Tynecastle. A lovely passing move slices open the Hearts defence and when Anthony Stokes finds Commons's run in the box, the former Derby County and Nottingham Forest midfielder hits a low shot across the keeper and into the bottom-right corner to put the Hoops 1-0 up.

28 September 2016

Celtic stun Pep Guardiola's Manchester City with a goal inside three minutes to send Parkhead wild with delight. Guardiola's City had a 100 per cent record going into this Group C Champions League group-stage clash, but the Celts are soon ahead as former City forward Scott Sinclair floats a free kick towards the back post which is volleyed back across by James Forrest, and Erik Sviatchenko's diving header hits Moussa Dembélé on its way past keeper Claudio Bravo into the back of the net the give the Hoops a 1-0 lead.

4

5 April 2006

John Hartson scores what will prove to be the goal that wraps up the SPL for the Celts. Up against nearest challengers Hearts at Parkhead, the Bhoys couldn't wish for a better start when Maciej Żurawski nods a long kick downfield from Artur Boruc to Hartson, who fires a shot from 25 yards that just evades the fingertips of Craig Gordon on its way into the back of the net. It will be the only goal of the game and ensures the Hoops cannot be caught.

26 March 2014

Celtic, needing a win to secure a third successive Scottish Premiership title, take the lead away to Partick Thistle with an Anthony Stokes header. Emilio Izaguirre is the creator, attacking down the left flank before cutting back on to his right foot and curling the ball into the Thistle box where Stokes heads home from a few yards out.

19 January 2016

Unmarked Mikael Lustig scores Celtic's first of eight goals against Hamilton as he rises to meet Stuart Armstrong's free kick from the left. The pace of the cross means Lustig – in acres of space in the six-yard box – need only connect for the ball to fly in the net and put Ronny Deila's side 1-0 up at Parkhead.

6 December 2016

Patrick Roberts returns to his parent club to score a stunning individual goal with only four minutes on the clock. Roberts, loaned to Celtic for the 2016/17 campaign, was given permission to play in the Champions League group-stage clash against Manchester City with the match at the Etihad effectively a 'dead rubber'. City had already qualified for the round of 16, whereas the Celts couldn't go any further following a largely disappointing qualification period, but Brendan Rodgers's side – who had already held City 3-3 at Parkhead – had a point to prove against Pep Guardiola's talented side. Roberts, out on the right flank, tricks his way past the City full-back before drawing in a couple more defenders and firing a superb, curling, left-foot shot past Willy Caballero to make it 1-0 for the Hoops.

5

1 September 1888

John O'Connor scores Celtic's first official goal as he bags an early strike against Shettleston in the Scottish Cup. Whether the 21-year-old realised the significance at the time is doubtful, but it would be a memorable day for the striker – if sketchy match reports are to be believed – as he would go on to score all five goals in the win at Celtic Park.

5 April 2014

Champions Celtic take the lead at Tannadice with a stunning volley from Georgios Samaras. Beram Kayal wins a free kick inside the Tangerines' half and Kris Commons angles it into the box for Samaras to beat Dundee United defender Gavin Gunning and volley the ball into the top corner of the net from ten yards to put the Celts 1-0 up.

6

16 April 1914

Jimmy McColl puts Celtic 1-0 up in the Scottish Cup Final against Hibs at Ibrox. The young striker's selection had surprised a few, so to get on the scoresheet so early in the game was a massive confidence booster. McColl's goal comes from a Browning corner, headed back across the six-yard box by McAtee and finished from close range by McColl.

28 October 1967

Stevie Chalmers nods Celtic into the lead against Dundee United in the Scottish League Cup Final. The Bhoys, chasing a third successive triumph in the competition, go ahead from a set piece as a corner is headed back towards the six-yard box for Chalmers to nod home from close range and make it 1-0 at Hampden Park.

26 October 1974

Jimmy Johnstone opens the scoring for Celtic in the Scottish League Cup Final at Hampden Park. The Hoops, hoping to avoid a fifth successive defeat in a League Cup final, get off to the perfect start when Jimmy Johnstone turns in a low cross from six yards out after excellent work from Kenny Dalglish on the left of the box to make it 1-0 over Hibs.

3 May 1986

What will be the start of an incredible final day in the 1985/86 SPL title race begins in earnest at Love Street. Hearts needed just a point to be crowned champions, while Celtic needed to win by at least three goals and hope the Jam Tarts went down at Dundee. Owen Archdeacon's corner is powerfully met by the head of a mullet-wearing Brian McClair to give Saints keeper Stewart no chance.

7 February 2001

Celtic strike first in the Old Firm Scottish League Cup semi-final at Hampden Park. Alan Thompson floats a free kick into the box and Ramon Vega sees his header thump off the Rangers crossbar, but Chris Sutton reacts quickest to volley high into the roof of the net from six yards and make it 1-0.

7

29 April 2017

Rangers' Myles Beerman needlessly fouls Patrick Roberts as Celtic are gifted a penalty at Ibrox. Roberts is chasing a ball out to the right when Beerman puts in a challenge on the corner of the box, clearly catching the winger just inside it. The referee consults his assistant before pointing to the spot and Scott Sinclair confidently dispatches the kick for the recently crowned Scottish Premiership champions to make it 1-0.

8 December 2020

Celtic take the lead in the San Siro thanks to some woeful AC Milan defending. Neil Lennon's side already know there is no way qualification from the Europa League group stages can be achieved, with just one point from a possible 15, but with pride at least to play for and with Milan trying (poorly) to play from the back and gifting the ball to Tom Rogic, his low left-foot shot into the bottom-left corner and beyond Gianluigi Donnarumma is superb.

8

16 April 1927

East Fife – the first second-tier side to reach the Scottish Cup Final in 30 years – had stunned Celtic with a goal shortly after kick-off to lead 1-0 at Hampden Park.

Celtic strike back almost immediately as Stewart Robertson becomes the second East Fife player to get his name on the scoresheet – but this time for putting through his own goal as his attempt to control a cross into the six-yard box sees the right-back instead knee the ball over his own goal line to make it 1-1.

11 September 1971

Lou Macari nods Celtic ahead at Ibrox from a set piece. Bobby Murdoch floats in a free kick from the right of the Rangers box and Macari – one of the smallest men on the pitch – heads home from close range to make it 1-0 in the Division One clash.

27 August 2000

Celtic again profit as an early Lubo Moravčík corner causes chaos and Stiliyan Petrov meets the cross with a header from close range thanks to more shocking Rangers defending. It puts Martin O'Neill's side 2-0 up in the Old Firm clash at Parkhead and on the way to an unforgettable victory.

4 May 2010

Lee Naylor's deflected free kick gives Celtic a 1-0 lead against already-crowned SPL champions Rangers. The free kick is awarded when Naismith scythes down Aiden McGeady 30 yards from goal. Naylor shapes up to take what looks like an ambitious shot but his low drive takes a sizeable deflection from Rangers captain David Weir eight yards from goal and diverts into the bottom-left corner to send Parkhead wild.

7 April 2012

Charlie Mulgrew heads Celtic into a 1-0 lead away to Kilmarnock, with a win guaranteeing a first SPL title for four years for the Hoops. The goal is from a set piece as Ki Sung-yueng's corner finds Mulgrew in the six-yard box and his header from close range gives the keeper no chance.

26 May 2013

Celtic, celebrating the club's 125th anniversary with a Scottish Cup Final appearance, take the lead against Hibernian at Hampden Park.

As a cross comes into the Hibs box, defender Alan Maybury's weak clearance allows Anthony Stokes to send in a superb deep cross from the left towards the back post out of the reach of keeper Ben Williams, and with defenders Paul Hanlon and Ryan McGivern ball-watching, Hooper squeezes the ball into the net to make it 1-0.

7 August 2016

James Forrest scores the first official Scottish Premiership goal of the Brendan Rodgers era at Celtic Park. In the opening-day clash against Hearts at Tynecastle, the Celts take just eight minutes to get the new manager's spell off and running as Callum McGregor is felled in the box and before the referee can point to the spot, Forrest sweeps home to start the Bhoys' title defence in style to make it 1-0.

9

15 April 1931

Taking full advantage of a strong wind behind them, fan favourite Bertie Thomson gets Celtic off to a great start in the 1931 Scottish Cup Final replay against Motherwell. A Hampden Park crowd in excess of 98,000 meant more than 200,000 fans had watched both games within the space of five days and this game would again be a thrilling spectacle. Thomson's opener comes after cutting in from the left and drilling the ball past the Well keeper.

12 April 1980

Bobby Lennox opens the scoring in the Scottish Cup semi-final against a Hibs side that counts the legendary former Manchester United star George Best among its starting XI. And what a goal it is, as Davie Provan bursts down the right flank before sending a deft chip into the box for Lennox to flick the ball past the keeper and put the Bhoys 1-0 up.

27 May 1995

Pierre van Hooijdonk grabs an early goal in the 110th Scottish Cup Final against Airdrie. When a cross from the right is scrambled clear, the ball finds its way to Tosh McKinlay who sends a deep cross into the box from the left and van Hooijdonk rises above his marker to powerfully head the ball into the bottom-left corner to score what will be the only goal of the game at Hampden Park.

19 January 2016

Nir Bitton doubles Celtic's lead against Hamilton. While Mikael Lustig's opener had all been about poor defending by the Accies, there is little that can be done as Bitton receives a pass 30 yards from goal and with nobody closing him down, he hits a swerving shot that ends in the right of the net to make it 2-0.

3 August 2019

Mikey Johnston gets the new campaign off to a cracking start with an excellent individual goal against St Johnstone. Ryan Christie plays a long angled pass to Johnston, who proceeds to torment the Saints right-back on his way to firing a low shot into the bottom-right corner from the left of the six-yard box.

10

18 April 1908

Alexander Bennett puts Celtic 1-0 up in the Scottish Cup Final against St Mirren. With more than 55,000 packed inside Hampden Park, Bennett's goal puts the Hoops on the way to a handsome victory.

28 October 1967

John Hughes scores a terrific individual goal to put Celtic into a 2-0 lead against Dundee United in the Scottish League Cup Final. Hughes chases a long ball forward on the right and outmuscles a United defender – but the ball is still loose and he has to go in hard to take possession, leaving another defender on the ground, before tucking a low shot past the keeper to double the Hoops' advantage.

1 February 2015

In the first Old Firm meeting for almost three years, Celtic take an early lead. The Hoops, facing Rangers at Hampden Park in the Scottish League Cup semi-final, open the scoring when Stefan Johansen sends in a cross from the right flank and Leigh Griffiths gets in between two Rangers defenders to head home from a few yards out to make it 1-0.

19 January 2016

Hamilton realise it's not going to be their day at Parkhead as they concede a third goal inside the opening ten minutes. A low cross from the right is partially cleared and eventually falls to Tom Rogic who sees his deflected shot from 18 yards give the keeper no chance.

11

16 April 1914

Jimmy McColl grabs his second of the game to put Celtic in command of the 1914 Scottish Cup Final. The young forward, who has scored after six minutes, hits a low shot on the run that the Hibs keeper fails to hold – McColl is first to the rebound, running between two defenders to place a low drive wide of the keeper in a game Celtic will go on to win 4-1 at Ibrox.

24 April 1937

Celtic take an early lead in a record-breaking Scottish Cup Final at Hampden Park. With 147,365 fans creating a new record for a club match, Johnny Crum puts the Bhoys ahead after the Aberdeen keeper parries Willie Buchan's shot to make it 1-0 – a lead that will last just 60 seconds before the Dons quickly level.

21 November 1998

Celtic take an early lead against Rangers in an Old Firm clash neither set of supporters want to miss. With almost 60,000 inside Parkhead and a further 30,000 watching on big screens at Ibrox to see if Rangers could extend their lead at the top, this felt like a must-win game for the Celts. When a low ball from Simon Donnelly is cleverly stepped over by Henrik Larsson, Lubo Moravčík hits a low shot into the bottom-right corner from the edge of the box to make it 1-0.

27 August 2000

Celtic fans are in dreamland as Paul Lambert makes it 3-0 against Rangers at Parkhead. Lubo Moravčík claims his third assist in 11 minutes as he drives into the Rangers box before stopping on the corner of the six-yard area and laying the ball into the path of the onrushing Lambert on the edge of the box, and he drills a powerful shot through a crowd of bodies to leave Rangers stunned.

28 May 2005

A somewhat fortuitous Celtic goal is enough to win the Scottish Cup Final against Dundee United. Craig Bellamy wins a free kick on the right of the Tangerines' box and Alan Thompson stands over the ball. With the expectation that Thompson will chip the ball into the six-yard box, he instead plays a low cross towards the near post, and as Bobo Baldé allows the ball to go through his legs, it clips the inside heel of United defender Garry Kenneth and rolls past his own keeper to make it 1-0 to the Hoops. It will be the only goal of the game and a fitting way to end the managerial tenure of Martin O'Neill, who had overseen seven major trophy successes during his stay at Celtic Park.

23 April 2017

Chasing a domestic treble, Brendan Rodgers's Celtic take an early lead over Rangers in the Scottish Cup semi-final at Hampden Park. The move that results in the opening goal is when Mikael Lustig's long pass finds Moussa Dembélé who brings the ball down, weighs up his options before spotting Callum McGregor's burst forward and lays it into his path. McGregor coolly places a shot into the bottom corner to make it 1-0.

27 May 2017

Celtic respond immediately to having gone 1-0 down to Aberdeen in the Scottish Cup Final. Looking to complete an unbeaten domestic treble, Brendan Rodgers's side show their mental strength as Callum McGregor shifts inside a challenge 30 yards from goal but as he is challenged, the referee plays advantage as Stuart Armstrong is given too much time to line up a low shot that he buries past the Dons keeper from 20 yards to make it 1-1 at Hampden Park.

11 March 2018

Tom Rogic levels for Celtic at Ibrox with a sumptuous 22-yard drive. Collecting the ball midway inside the Rangers half, Rogic heads towards the box, drifting slightly more to the centre before unleashing a curling left-foot drive into the top-right corner to make it 1-1 in an explosive start to the Scottish Premiership Old Firm clash.

19 May 2018

Celtic take the lead with a stunning effort from Callum McGregor to put the Hoops 1-0 up in the Scottish Cup Final against Motherwell. Mikael Lustig's cross from the right is headed out of the box, but it is McGregor who is more alert and he races between two Well players to claim possession and then sends a sweet half-volley into the top right-hand corner of Trevor Carson's net from 18 yards.

12

21 April 1951

Celtic end a 13-year wait for silverware by landing a 16th Scottish Cup success with a hard-fought 1-0 win over Motherwell. Watched by a huge crowd of 131,943 fans at Hampden Park, the Bhoys take an early lead through a strike worthy of winning any cup final. John McPhail's superb control takes him away from two Motherwell defenders and his deft chip over the advancing Johnstone sends the majority of the crowd wild – and it will prove to be the only goal of the game.

27 February 2003

Leading 3-1 from the UEFA Cup fourth round first leg at Parkhead, Celtic get an early goal in the return leg in Germany against Stuttgart. Didier Agathe sends a high, dipping cross into the box that John Hartson flicks on for Alan Thompson to head into the corner of the net to make it 1-0 on the night and 4-1 on aggregate.

13

7 December 1966

Jinky Johnstone opens the scoring against Nantes in the European Cup second round second-leg tie at Parkhead to put Jock Stein's men 4-1 up on aggregate. Johnstone glides through the French side's rearguard before drilling a low shot home to make it 1-0 on the night.

5 November 2008

Celtic Park goes wild as the Bhoys take an early lead against European champions Manchester United in a Champions League group-stage clash in Glasgow. The Celts press for the advantage and after a game of head tennis, Gary Caldwell cushions a header towards Scott McDonald on his left and McDonald chests the ball down before sending a sublime half-volley lob over Ben Foster.

14

3 May 1975

On an emotional day at Hampden Park, Celtic take an early lead against Airdrie. The 1975 Scottish Cup Final was to be skipper Billy McNeill's final game for the club and the Hoops were determined he should go out on a high. Kenny Dalglish is at the heart of the move that results in the opening goal when he plays it out wide, before running into space and collecting a return ball on the right of the Airdrie box. Dalglish then clips a perfect cross into the box for Paul Wilson to nod home from close range, much to the delight of the majority of the sun-drenched Hampden Park crowd – and you can't say that too often!

10 December 2009

Shaun Maloney heads Celtic into a 1-0 lead against Villarreal in the final Champions League group-stage clash at Parkhead. The goal comes when Mark Wilson gets into the Spaniards' box before crossing into the six-yard area, where keeper Sebastián Viera makes a hash of trying to catch the ball and Maloney rises at the back post to head home.

29 April 2018

With a dream scenario of clinching a seventh successive title with victory over Rangers, Celtic start what will be an unbelievable day with a goal on 14. Kieran Tierney takes on Daniel Candeias and glides past with ease before firing a low cross in that Odsonne Édouard expertly tucks into the bottom-right corner from close range to put Brendan Rodgers's side on the way.

8 December 2020

More poor defending by AC Milan who concede again in the Europa League tie with Celtic. The Celts, already eliminated at the group stage, at least make a fist of it as Édouard runs on to Ryan Christie's pass to delicately lift the ball over Gianluigi Donnarumma to make it 2-0 to Neil Lennon's men at the San Siro – a game in which the Italians will come back strongly to win 4-2.

30 September 2001

When Celtic win a free kick some 25 yards from the Rangers goal and to the left of the box, Henrik Larsson and Stiliyan Petrov stand over the ball. After lining up the wall, the referee blows and Petrov runs up and hits it through the wall and Rangers keeper Stefan Klos makes a hash of attempting to save the shot which bounces off his knee and into the back of the net to give the Hoops a precious 1-0 lead at Ibrox.

15

16 April 1927

Adam McLean puts Celtic 2-1 up in the Scottish Cup Final against East Fife as the goals continue to flow at Hampden Park. With the rest of Scotland willing the second-tier Fife side to cause an upset, Celtic show their class as Paddy Connolly's cross is turned home by McLean to round off a superb passing move from the Hoops.

14 November 2002

Celtic get a vital away goal in the UEFA Cup second-round second leg at Ewood Park. Having edged past Blackburn Rovers 1-0 in the first leg, the Celts need the comfort of an away goal and who else but Henrik Larsson should deliver? Didier Agathe's short ball to Chris Sutton is helped on by the former Rovers striker and as John Hartson and Craig Short move towards the ball, they both slip, allowing Larsson to take over. As the keeper rushes out, the Swede calmly dinks the ball over him and into the net to make it 1-0.

19 March 2000

A goal created by Scandinavia as Celtic take the lead against Aberdeen in the 2000 Scottish League Cup Final at Hampden Park. Dane Morten Wieghorst collects a short pass on the left of the Dons box before sliding a low cross into the edge of the six-yard box, and Norwegian Vidar Riseth manages to poke the ball through the legs of goalkeeper Jim Leighton to make it 1-0.

27 February 2003

Didier Agathe claims his second assist in four minutes to virtually assure Celtic of progression into the UEFA Cup quarter-finals. Agathe speeds past Timo Wenzel before crossing low across the box for Chris Sutton to tap home and make it 2-0 on the night and 5-1 on aggregate – and even though Stuttgart rally to win 3-2, they are still two goals short of going into the last eight.

16

25 August 2001

Lubo Moravčík fires Celtic ahead against Hibs at Easter Road with a stunning goal. The Slovakian is 25 yards out when he just decides to let fly with an angled howitzer of a shot that arrows into the top-right corner of the net to make it 1-0 to the Celts.

20 February 2008

Jan Vennegoor of Hesselink heads Celtic into the lead against Barcelona to lift the roof of Parkhead. Barca, containing a 20-year-old Lionel Messi, are shaken when Scott McDonald battles for the ball in the Catalans' box, before managing to find Lee Naylor on the left of the box – his first-time cross finds Dutch striker Hesselink who thumps his header past Víctor Valdés from six yards.

27 November 2016

Tom Rogic opens the scoring in the Scottish League Cup Final with a superb goal. Jozo Šimunović plays a key role, forging towards the Dons box before sliding a pass out to Rogic on the right of the box. The Australian cuts inside before lashing a left-foot shot into the bottom-left corner of the net to set the Hoops on the way at Hampden Park.

17

7 February 2001

Celtic go 2-0 up against Rangers in the Scottish League Cup semi-final at Hampden Park. Henrik Larsson chases a high ball towards the Rangers box and young defender Robert Malcolm desperately tries to hold off the Swede but is quickly overpowered as Larsson outmuscles him before just getting to the ball before keeper Stefan Klos, lobbing it over his head, rounding him and then gently volleying it into the empty net to double the Hoops' lead.

25 August 2001

Rampant Celtic score a second goal in two minutes as Chris Sutton profits from some shocking Hibs defending. An attempted pass back towards goal by a Hibs defender only puts a colleague under pressure and as the ball comes down on the edge of the box, a determined Sutton uses his strength to win possession before drilling a low shot past the keeper to put the Hoops 2-0 up at Easter Road.

20 February 2011

Celtic strike the first blow in the Old Firm meeting with Rangers at Parkhead in what is also a crucial SPL title clash. After moving the ball around the pitch, play switches to the left flank and Kris Commons spots Gary Hooper just outside the box – he plays a low pass in and Hooper's first touch sees him dart between two defenders before firing a low drive through Allan McGregor's legs.

6 February 2011

Kris Commons, having scored on his Celtic debut, scores on his Old Firm debut to level the scores at Ibrox. Trailing from a third-minute Rangers goal and having seen the hosts also strike the underside of the crossbar, a ball is deflected into the path of Joe Ledley and his low cross across the box is hammered home by Commons to make it 1-1 in a frenetic Scottish Cup fifth-round tie.

7 April 2012

Having scored the opener, Charlie Mulgrew, playing at left-back but on the right of the Kilmarnock box, sends in the perfect cross towards the back post where Glenn Loovens escapes Mahamadou Sissoko to powerfully send an angled header past the keeper to make it 2-0.

18

23 October 1965

Celtic's bid to end an eight-year drought of silverware gets off to a good start when Rangers' Ron McKinnon needlessly gives away a penalty in the Scottish League Cup Final at Hampden Park. Roared on by a colossal crowd of 107,609 – a record for a League Cup final in the UK – the referee has the simple decision of pointing to the spot. John Hughes steps up to send the Rangers keeper Billy Ritchie the wrong way and make it 1-0 for the Bhoys.

19 April 2015

Virgil van Dijk keeps Celtic on track for a domestic treble as he opens the scoring in the Scottish Cup semi-final against Inverness Caledonian Thistle at Hampden Park. The Dutch defender steps up to take a free kick on the edge of the box and clips a shot over the wall and in off the left post to make it 1-0. A superb free kick.

29 April 2017

Leigh Griffiths doubles Celtic's lead at Ibrox in double quick time. Rangers are again their own worst enemy as Emerson Hyndman loses possession in his own half to Stuart Armstrong, who then plays a pass out to Griffiths who runs towards goal at an angle before unleashing a ferocious drive that flies across the keeper and into the top-right corner to put the champions 2-0 up.

19

29 October 1966

Celtic successfully defend the Scottish League Cup by again beating Rangers narrowly. The Bhoys had won 2-1 a year before and in front of another huge Hampden Park crowd of 94,532, Bobby Lennox grabs the only goal of the game – and what a superb goal it is. Bertie Auld's fine cross to the back post is headed back across the box by Joe McBride and without breaking stride, Lennox thumps a sumptuous volley past Martin in the Rangers goal to score and ensure the trophy heads back to Celtic Park for the fifth time in what will be a momentous season for the club.

30 October 1982

Paul McStay levels the scores at Celtic Park in a Scottish Premier League clash with Rangers. Murdo MacLeod races into the box and sees his shot parried by onrushing keeper Jim Stewart – but only into the path of teenager Paul McStay, who has the simplest of tasks to tap the ball into the empty net to make it 1-1.

20 December 2020

Ryan Christie puts Celtic ahead in stunning fashion in the delayed Scottish Cup Final at Hampden Park. The ball arrives at Christie's feet on the edge of the Hearts box courtesy of a poor clearance and after moving slightly inside with his first touch, he curls a superb 25-yard shot over former team-mate Craig Gordon with his second to put the Bhoys ahead and keep Neil Lennon's side on track for a historic quadruple treble.

20

8 March 1972

Celtic go ahead in the European Cup quarter-final against Újpest Dozsa in Hungary. In dreadful conditions after torrential rain, Jim Brogan's long ball towards the Hungarians' box is turned past his own keeper by Horváth to give the Bhoys a valuable 1-0 lead in the first leg.

4 May 1974

Celtic take a 1-0 lead in the Scottish Cup Final against Dundee United. The opening goal comes when Dixie Deans lobs a pass into the path of Harry Hood who outpaces two defenders and as United keeper Sandy Davie races off his line, Hood nods the ball over the keeper and into the net to send much of the 75,959 Hampden Park crowd into celebration.

7 May 1977

With a crowd of 54,000 one of the lowest in Scottish Cup final memory – partly due to bad weather and the first live TV screening of the game since 1955 – Celtic take the lead after a hotly disputed penalty when Rangers' Derek Johnstone is adjudged to have handled on the goal line. The referee waves away protests and after elected taker Kenny Dalglish declines, Andy Lynch steps up to take the spot kick, tucking the ball into the bottom right-hand corner to score the only goal of the game and secure Jock Stein's 25th trophy as manager.

25 August 2001

Celtic continue a blistering start at Easter Road with a third goal in five minutes against Hibs. Lubo Moravčík is again involved as he chips a pass into the path of Chris Sutton who again uses his speed and strength to get in behind the increasingly beleaguered Hibs defence to slide a low shot across the keeper and into the bottom-left corner to make it 3-0 at Easter Road.

28 March 2004

Rangers' hopes of catching Celtic in the SPL title race are finally ended on another 'Beachball Sunday' at Ibrox. The Gers have a chance to reduce the gap to 13 points and a glimmer of hope, but they will end the day 19 points adrift of the Bhoys, who grab the lead when Alan Thompson's free kick sees Henrik Larsson ghost in behind defender Michael Ball to head home from close range.

16 April 2008

In a game the Celts have to win to keep hopes of another SPL title alive, Shunsuke Nakamura scores a spectacular long-range effort over Allan McGregor who is a few yards off his line to make it 1-0 against Rangers. Gary Caldwell pings a ball infield to Nakamura who is more than 30 yards out when he unleashes a viciously swerving shot that rockets into the top-left corner. Cue pandemonium!

28 September 2016

In an explosive start to the Group C Champions League group-stage clash with Manchester City, Celtic retake the lead at Parkhead – and deservedly so. Pep Guardiola's side had fought back from going behind to Moussa Dembélé's third-minute goal but the Bhoys go ahead again as Tom Rogic finds Kieran Tierney's run into the box and the youngster's low shot is deflected past Claudio Bravo to make it 2-1.

21

30 November 1997

Celtic get the breakthrough against Dundee United in the 1997 Scottish League Cup Final at Ibrox. The Hoops, without a final victory since 1982, attack down the right flank and Morten Wieghorst's cross into the middle is met by the head of Marc Rieper who sees his effort smack the left post before going into the back of the net to make it 1-0.

13 September 2006

Jan Vennegoor of Hesselink puts Celtic 1-0 up away to Manchester United in the Champions League group-stage clash at Old Trafford. Artur Boruc's long punt upfield sees Vennegoor of Hesselink outmuscle Rio Ferdinand, bring the ball down and spin away before burying a low left-foot shot past Edwin van der Sar to stun the Stretford End.

7 November 2012

The roof nearly comes off Celtic Park as the Bhoys take a 1-0 lead over Barcelona in the Champions League group-stage clash in Glasgow. The Catalans – with Lionel Messi in their ranks – have struggled from set pieces and when Charlie Mulgrew's right-flank corner is floated towards the far side of the six-yard box, Victor

Wanyama rises to head powerfully past Víctor Valdés to give the Hoops the lead.

1 December 2013

Quick-thinking Charlie Mulgrew catches Hearts' defence asleep as he plays a short free kick into the box, which Kris Commons races on to and fires a powerful angled drive into the top-left corner to put the Celts 2-0 up at Tynecastle in the Scottish Cup fourth round. The Hearts players had been expecting a ball to be floated in from the right when Mulgrew catches them organising for a set piece that never comes.

15 May 2016

Newly crowned champions Celtic take the lead in what is manager Ronny Deila's final match in charge of the Bhoys. In the final Scottish Premiership game of the season, Kieran Tierney – outstanding all season – starts what will be a very long afternoon for Motherwell as he cuts in from the left, beats a defender and then buries a low right-foot drive into the bottom-left corner to make it 1-0 at Parkhead.

22

19 October 1957

Celtic draw first blood in the first major Old Firm final for 30 years, with Rangers the opposition at Hampden Park for the Scottish League Cup Final. The Bhoys could be four up by the time the deadlock is finally broken, as McPhail's nod down is thumped home on the volley by Sammy Wilson to send at least half of the 82,000+ crowd into raptures.

5 October 1966

Tommy Gemmell scores the all-important away goal Celtic need in the European Cup first-round second-leg tie against Zurich. Gemmell, who scored a stunning goal in the first leg, puts the Hoops 3-0 up on aggregate as he again thunders home an unstoppable 30-yard shot to confirm his reputation as one of the best attacking left-backs in Europe.

19 January 2016

Gary Mackay-Steven drives into the Hamilton box after an excellent run before playing a short pass to his left where Leigh Griffiths buries an angled shot past the Hamilton keeper to put the Celts 4-0 up at Parkhead. Unfortunately for the Accies, it's only half of the number of goals they will eventually concede ...

15 April 2018

Celtic take the initiative in the Scottish Cup semi-final against Rangers at Hampden Park with a goal that is typical of Tom Rogic's tenacity and skill. Moussa Dembélé picks the ball up on the right of the Rangers box before playing it back to James Forrest who immediately lays it square to Rogic. The Australian swivels one way, then with a Cruyff-like turn he switches direction before planting a low shot past the keeper from eight yards to make it 1-0.

23

1 November 1967

Jinky Johnstone wins a penalty kick in the tinderbox atmosphere of the World Club Championship second leg against Racing Club in Buenos Aires. The first leg in Glasgow had seen a number of disgraceful tackles, punches and headbutts from the Argentines but Johnstone's trickery allows Tommy Gemmell to step up and just squeeze the ball past Agustín Cejas to put the Celts 1-0 up on the day and 2-0 up on aggregate – but the hosts will score either side of half-time to force a replay, with away goals not counting double at the time.

5 April 1969

Willie Wallace puts Celtic ahead in the Scottish League Cup Final. The game had been delayed six months due to a fire at Hampden Park, hence the unusual April scheduling, but it made no difference to the Hoops who were chasing a fourth successive final success in the competition. In front of another huge crowd, Celtic open the scoring when Hibs fail to clear a free kick from the right and the ball eventually falls to Wallace on the edge of the box and his fierce low drive finds the bottom corner of the net.

6 May 1972

Having seen their early advantage pegged back by Hibs, Celtic regain the lead in the Scottish Cup Final – and it is another set piece that undoes the Edinburgh men as Bobby Murdoch's free kick from the right is headed home by John 'Dixie' Deans to make it 2-1.

4 December 1982

Celtic take the lead over Rangers in the Scottish League Cup Final. It has been eight years since the Hoops won the trophy, but a superb opening goal sets the tone for a pulsating Old Firm encounter at Hampden Park. David Provan cuts in from the right flank before nudging the ball on to Charlie Nicholas on the edge of the box, and his clever first-time shot catches the keeper off guard on its way into the bottom right of the Rangers net.

24

30 November 1966

Celtic equalise in the European Cup second-round first-leg tie away to French side Nantes. The hosts have taken the lead on 16 minutes, but the Hoops respond quickly with a well-crafted goal as Joe McBride receives a pass just inside the box, sidesteps his marker, and drills a low shot past the keeper from 15 yards to make it 1-1.

29 May 1971

Three weeks after the first game had been played, the Scottish Cup Final was replayed at a packed and passionate Hampden Park as Celtic and Rangers resumed battle. It is the Gers who start brighter, going close on a couple of occasions, before the Hoops take the lead with the simplest of goals as Bobby Lennox's low corner is dummied by Billy McNeill and finds its way to youngster Lou Macari, who plants the ball home from six yards with a swing of the left boot to send one end of the famous old stadium into raptures.

4 May 1974

Celtic take a commanding 2-0 lead in the 1974 Scottish Cup Final over Dundee United with a second goal in four minutes. A scramble in the United box sees the ball fall to Jimmy Johnstone and his touch rolls into the path of Steve Murray. The midfielder buries a low shot past Sandy Davie to double the Hoops' lead.

30 November 1997

Henrik Larsson scores Celtic's second goal in less than three minutes to give the Hoops a commanding early lead over Dundee United in the Scottish League Cup Final at Ibrox. The Swede advances towards the Tangerines' box before deciding to have a punt from 25 yards – the shot deflects off a United defender and loops up and over the keeper to make it 2-0 and put his side firmly on course for victory.

31 October 2001

Though Celtic couldn't end a first Champions League group stage adventure with a place in the round of 16, this final match against the already-qualified Juventus offered more valuable experience for Martin O'Neill's side. Despite having gone behind on 19 minutes, the Celts are soon level as Lubo Moravčík's cross is met by Belgian defender Joos Valgaeren, who heads home spectacularly from 12 yards to make it 1-1 at Parkhead.

18 February 2006

Dunfermline Athletic fans are no doubt quite happy as the first half reaches its halfway point with the score 1-1 and their side very much in the game. But, they couldn't have envisaged that the Celts would add seven unanswered goals in the time that remained, starting with a John Hartson strike. After Maciej Żurawski has seen his shot saved, Hartson is first to pounce on the loose ball with a powerful drive into the roof of the net.

5 April 2014

Anthony Stokes makes it 2-0 for the Hoops away to Dundee United. The second goal is the result of a superb team move that ends when Stokes plays a clever one-two with Kris Commons before moving past a couple of United defenders and finishing with a rising shot past keeper Radosław Cierzniak. That will end the scoring at Tannadice and put Celtic 28 points clear of second-placed Aberdeen.

19 February 2015

Celtic, stunned by two early Inter Milan goals in the Europa League round of 32 first-leg tie at Parkhead, at last get a foothold in the game with a well-worked goal. Stefan Johansen plays the ball wide to Adam Matthews who gets to the right of the Inter box before putting a low cross into the middle, where Stuart Armstrong arrives to power a low shot home and make it 1-2 in Inter's favour.

2 April 2017

On a day Celtic can clinch a sixth successive title Hearts do their best to deny the Bhoys with a spirited first 20 minutes or so. But the breakthrough comes with a super goal with strong Manchester City connections as former City forward Scott Sinclair plays a pass to on-loan City winger Patrick Roberts on the left of the Hearts box. Sinclair then accelerates into the box where Roberts returns the pass and Sinclair hits a ferocious angled shot into the roof of the net to put the champions-elect ahead at Tynecastle.

25

29 May 1971

Having just fallen behind in the Old Firm Scottish Cup Final replay, Rangers make an awful hash of trying to clear another Celtic attack. Three Rangers players get in a muddle on the edge of their own box before the ball is passed to Jimmy Johnstone in the box and as he skips around defender Ron McKinnon, he is rugby-tackled to the ground and the referee points to the spot. Harry Hood hits the spot kick crisply to the right of the keeper to double the Hoops' lead – an advantage Celtic will see over the line to record a 2-1 win, a 21st Scottish Cup success and Jock Stein's 16th trophy as manager.

19 February 2015

It's two goals in two minutes as Celtic recover from 2-0 down to make it 2-2 against Inter Milan in a pulsating Europa League round of 32 first-leg tie at Parkhead. Straight after pulling one back, the Celts go again at the Italian defence and when a throw-in finds Stefan Johansen, his lob into the box causes panic on the near post and as a result, Campagnaro prods past his own keeper to make it 2-2.

19 May 2018

Celtic go 2-0 up against Motherwell in the Scottish Cup Final to put one hand firmly on the oldest domestic trophy in Britain. Leading through Callum McGregor's sweet strike on 11, the Bhoys double the lead when Moussa Dembélé holds the ball up before feeding Olivier Ntcham who drills a low shot past keeper Trevor Carson. It will be enough to secure victory and a magnificent treble success for the second year running – a domestic 'double treble' in fact for Brendan Rodgers's all-conquering side.

26

6 November 2010

Celtic open the scoring against Aberdeen when Dons skipper Paul Hartley handles Ki Sung-yeung's goal-bound shot and is shown a straight red card as a result after the referee points to the spot. Stokes sends the keeper the wrong way to make it 1-0 at Parkhead.

15 May 2016

Celtic double the lead against Motherwell on the final day of the 2015/16 Scottish Premiership season. Already crowned champions, the Bhoys are determined to end Ronny Deila's tenure on a high and Stuart Armstrong is integral in the second goal of the afternoon at Parkhead, playing a neat one-two with Ryan Christie on the edge of the box before sending a measured shot past the keeper – but it strikes the foot of the post and Tom Rogic is on hand to tap home his easiest goal of the campaign.

3 August 2019

Celtic double the lead in their Scottish Premiership curtain-raiser against St Johnstone at Parkhead. James Forrest picks out Ryan Christie on the edge of the Saints box and Christie curls a shot past the keeper from 20 yards to open his account for the season and put the Celts 2-0 up.

27

12 April 1967

With Parkhead bursting at the seams, the Hoops take the lead in the European Cup semi-final first leg. Though an earlier goal has been disallowed, there is no argument from the Dukla Prague players as Stevie Chalmers cleverly slips Jinky Johnstone in, and the diminutive winger just manages to lift the ball over Viktor the keeper and into the net before colliding with him as almost 75,000 fans go wild.

29 August 2007

Celtic take the lead on the night and on aggregate as Scott McDonald makes it 1-0 against Spartak Moscow. With a place in the Champions League group stage at stake, Roman Shishkin's poor clearance falls straight to McDonald who tucks home from 12 yards.

2 April 2017

The same combination that had created Celtic's opening goal just three minutes earlier repeat the formula as Celtic double the lead against Hearts. Needing a win to secure the Scottish Premiership title, Patrick Roberts receives a pass just inside the Hearts half and he then plays a precise through ball to Scott Sinclair who uses his pace to race clear and thump a powerful shot past the keeper from eight yards to put his side 2-0 up at Tynecastle.

31 March 2019

Odsonne Édouard receives a pass just past the halfway line and proceeds towards the Rangers goal. Édouard cuts slightly inside as he is pursued by defenders before dropping his shoulder, moving the ball to his left and firing a rising shot past the keeper and into the middle of the net to make it 1-0 at Parkhead.

28

23 October 1965

Celtic are awarded a second penalty in the Scottish League Cup Final at Hampden Park. There seems little danger when Jinky Johnstone collects the ball on the right flank – but despite the close attentions of Rangers defender David Provan, Johnstone spins around, beats his man and heads towards the box where Provan's desperate challenge brings the Hoops' legendary winger down. The referee points to the spot and John Hughes steps up to take it – this time, he chooses the bottom-right corner and keeper Billy Ritchie gets a good hand to it, but can't keep it out and Celtic take a 2-0 lead that will eventually prove enough to win the game 2-1 and end an eight-year wait for silverware.

6 November 2010

Gary Hooper makes it two goals in three minutes for the Hoops who go 2-0 up against ten-man Aberdeen at Parkhead. Hooper uses his strength to outmuscle Zander Diamond on the edge of the box before finishing smartly past keeper Langfield from just inside the box.

20 February 2011

Gary Hooper doubles Celtic's lead against Rangers to put Neil Lennon's side firmly in command in the Old

Firm clash at Parkhead. The Celts counter-attack with Georgios Samaras and as the Greek forward advances, he spots Emilio Izaguirre's surging run on the left, plays a perfect pass into his path and Izaguirre plays a first-time low cross into the six-yard box for Hooper to finish from close range and make it 2-0.

15 March 2015

Celtic go ahead against Dundee United in the Scottish League Cup Final. Kris Commons arrives perfectly to meet a cross that is initially well saved by Tangerines keeper Radosław Cierzniak but Commons reacts quickest to the loose ball, sweeping home from a couple of yards out to put the Hoops 1-0 up.

15 May 2016

Motherwell's day – and in particular that of their goalkeeper's – gets worse as the Hoops score a third goal in eight minutes to open up a 3-0 lead at Parkhead. As Stuart Armstrong's deep corner clears Connor Ripley's attempted clearance, Mikael Lustig cleverly heads downwards past two defenders to put the champions on the way to a handsome victory.

29

27 April 2003

Alan Thompson puts Celtic ahead in a game dubbed 'Beachball Sunday' at Ibrox. Having weathered a considerable early storm from Rangers who have missed several gilt-edged chances to go ahead, John Hartson skips past Lorenzo Amoruso and is felled in the box as the pair tangle. The referee points to the spot and Thompson, cool as you like, takes a sizeable run-up before sending the keeper the wrong way to put Celtic 1-0 up – much to the delight of the beach-dressed thousands of travelling fans at the opposite end of the ground.

15 May 2011

On a day when Celtic know a victory and Rangers failing to win at Kilmarnock will see the SPL title go to Parkhead rather than Ibrox, Gary Hooper breaks the deadlock against Motherwell. The visitors, with a Scottish Cup Final to come a week later, have made a number of changes but the Celts – perhaps sensing the inevitable at Rugby Park – have held on until a ball into the box finds Hooper and after the Well defence fail to clear his first attempt, Hooper prods the loose ball home to make it 1-0. The Hoops fans already know Rangers have raced into a 3-0 lead against Killie, meaning the race is all but over.

20 December 2020

Odsonne Édouard makes Hearts pay for a handball in the box from a corner. As the ball sails into the area, it clearly strikes Christophe Berra's high arm and the referee immediately points to the spot. Calm and cool as ever, Édouard steps up and dinks a Panenka-style spot kick over Gordon to double the Hoops' lead in the coronavirus-delayed Scottish Cup Final.

30

6 April 1912

James McMenemy opens the scoring against Clyde in the Scottish Cup Final after Clyde's Gilligan slips to let in the Hoops forward who makes no mistake. Celtic go on to win the game 2-0 at Ibrox, watched by more than 50,000 spectators. It is the eighth time Celtic have been crowned Scottish Cup champions.

15 April 1931

Jimmy McGrory restores Celtic's lead against Motherwell in the 1931 Scottish Cup Final replay at Hampden Park. The Well had equalised just four minutes earlier through Johnny Murdoch, but McGrory's effort on the half hour makes it 2-1 for the Bhoys.

5 April 1969

Celtic double the lead in the Scottish League Cup Final. The goal is the result of an almighty goalmouth scramble, caused by Stevie Chalmers's mazy run into the box and low cross with Hibs desperately blocking a couple of close-range shots, before the ball falls to Bertie Auld who plants a right-foot shot high into the right of the net to make it 2-0 at Hampden Park.

6 May 1970

On a night when Jock Stein claimed that too many of his stars had an off-night, Celtic take the lead in the European Cup Final against Feyenoord. Though the Dutch side will fight back to win 2-1 in extra time, the Bhoys send 20,000 travelling fans wild in Milan with a typically well-worked free kick. Awarded a foul on the edge of the Feyenoord box, Bobby Murdoch shapes up to have a crack at goal and as he runs up at speed, that's exactly what looks likely to happen – but it's all a ruse and as he gets to take strike, Murdoch cleverly reverses the ball to Tommy Gemmell just behind and the Celtic left-back sends a missile of a shot through the wall and past the keeper to make it 1-0 and seemingly put his side on their way ... At least Gemmell joins an exclusive group of players to have scored in two European Cup finals, though this was little more than a consolation for a side that had been favourites to win the game.

1 May 2015

Emilio Izaguirre is given plenty of time to size up and then deliver a fine cross from the left flank that Leigh Griffiths rises to head past the keeper to put the Celts 1-0 up over Dundee at Parkhead. Needing victory to all but seal the Scottish Premiership title, it will be the first of a five-goal rout for Celtic.

3 August 2019

James Forrest claims his second assist of the game as Celtic go 3-0 up against St Johnstone. And it is Ryan Christie who is again the beneficiary as he collects Forrest's simple pass back to the edge of the box for Christie to drill a low left-foot shot that Saints keeper Clark makes an awful hash of, misjudging the power of the drive on what will be a long afternoon for the Perth side at Parkhead.

31

24 April 1965

Celtic draw level in the Scottish Cup Final against a dogged and determined Dunfermline Athletic. Charlie Gallacher's shot hits the crossbar, loops up in the air and Bertie Auld's leap sees him beat a defender and head the rebound home to make it 1-1 in front of 108,000 Hampden Park fans.

4 December 1982

Murdo MacLeod's howitzer of a shot into the top-right corner doubles Celtic's lead in the Scottish Cup Final. Rangers half clear a corner kick back out to the right flank – the deep cross is again only half cleared to the edge of the box where MacLeod runs in and lashes a fierce shot past keeper Stewart to make it 2-0 and send half of Hampden Park wild. It will be enough to ensure the Hoops win the game 2-1 and win the trophy for the ninth time.

25 August 2001

Henrik Larsson rises to head home Alan Thompson's corner as Celtic continue to dismantle Hibs at Easter Road. It's a simple set-piece goal that gives the Hoops a 4-0 lead in the SPL clash with barely half an hour on the clock.

12 August 1989

When a corner comes in from the right, Roy Aitken is clearly pushed to the floor by a Hearts defender and the referee points to the spot. Tommy Coyne steps up to take the penalty and squeezes a shot past the keeper in off the post to make it 1-0 for the Celts at Tynecastle in the SPL.

1 February 2015

Rangers fail to clear the danger and Kris Commons hits a rocket shot into the top-left corner from 20 yards out to double Celtic's advantage in the Scottish League Cup semi-final at Hampden Park. It's a superb strike from Commons and his effort will secure a place in the final for Ronny Deila's side with no further scoring in the game.

26 May 2013

The same combination that had created Celtic's opening goal against Hibs repeats the feat to give the Hoops a 2-0 lead in the Scottish Cup Final. Anthony Stokes again sends in a superb cross from the left and Gary Hooper rises high to nod the ball down into the ground and past the keeper to score his 31st goal of the campaign – in the 31st minute!

32

3 May 1986

Celtic's slim SPL title hopes take a further boost with a second goal against St Mirren. Needing victory by three goals and Hearts to get beat, Paul McStay sends Mo Johnston clear and his scuffed shot from just inside the box bobbles past the keeper into the bottom-left corner to make it 2-0 at Love Street. But there was much more to come 60 seconds later ...

18 February 2006

Maciej Żurawski scores his first of four goals in the rout over Dunfermline Athletic. John Hartson plays a threaded pass into Żuwraski's run and from slightly left of centre, the Polish striker thumps a rising left-foot shot across the keeper and into the right-hand corner to put the Celts 3-1 up.

21 May 2011

Ki Sung-yueng fires an absolute howitzer of a shot from more than 30 yards out to put Celtic 1-0 up against Motherwell in the Scottish Cup Final. The South Korean collects a pass midway inside the Well half and with space ahead of him he sends a bullet of a left-foot shot into the bottom-left corner of the net for a stunning goal.

1 September 2019

Celtic open the scoring at Ibrox with a goal caused by poor Rangers defending. Connor Goldson's wayward pass is picked up by Mikey Johnston, who drives towards the Rangers box before slipping a pass through to Odsonne Édouard who coolly slides a shot under the keeper to put Neil Lennon's side in control in the first Scottish Premiership clash of the 2019/20 campaign.

33

3 May 1986

Celtic fans suddenly start to dream that the seemingly impossible might actually happen – and it's a goal worthy of champions, too. The ball is cleared out of the Celtic defence and Danny McGrain carries it over the halfway line before nudging it to Brian McClair on the right. McClair nutmegs the full-back before sending a low cross towards the back post where Mo Johnston slides home his second in two minutes to make it 3-0 against St Mirren. As things stand, if leaders Hearts were to lose at Dundee, the Hoops would win the SPL.

6 November 2010

The Celts make it three goals in eight minutes against ten-man Aberdeen. The visitors' nightmare afternoon had begun when skipper Paul Hartley had been dismissed for deliberate handball, opening the floodgates for the rampant Hoops. Niall McGinn cuts in from the right and Zander Diamond's attempt to clear a near-post cross ends with the ball falling at the feet of Gary Hooper, who makes no mistake from close range to make it 3-0 in the SPL clash at Parkhead and score his second of the afternoon.

10 September 2016

Moussa Dembélé scores the first of what will be a memorable hat-trick against Rangers at Parkhead. In the first Scottish Premiership Old Firm clash for four years, Dembélé rises to power home Scott Sinclair's corner and put the Celts 1-0 up on a sunny Glasgow afternoon.

34

15 April 1931

Bertie Thompson scores his second – and Celtic's third – to put the Bhoys firmly in control of the Scottish Cup Final replay at Hampden. It is a second goal in the space of four minutes to knock the stuffing out of Motherwell who had levelled on 26 minutes and, of course, had thrown a two-goal lead away in the final eight minutes in the first meeting five days earlier.

26 October 1974

Pat McCluskey moves forward from his own half before playing a superb pass that splits the Hibs defence apart, and Dixie Deans runs on to the ball and lifts it over the onrushing keeper from the edge of the box to double Celtic's lead in the Scottish League Cup Final at Hampden Park. With the score 2-0 with just over half an hour played, it already looks like a long way back for the Edinburgh men.

1 December 2013

Scott Brown scores the simplest goal of his career against Hearts and celebrates in front of the home fans who regularly remind him of his days with Edinburgh rivals Hibs. It's a smart move that sees Anthony Stokes control a long ball before waiting for Joe Ledley's overlap

– Ledley's low shot is pushed on to the post and Brown is on hand to tap home into the unguarded net to put the Bhoys 3-0 up at Tynecastle and on the way to the next round of the Scottish Cup.

19 January 2016

Hamilton's defending goes from bad to worse as the Bhoys score a fifth before half-time. After initially scrambling Tom Rogic's cross clear, Rogic collects the loose ball on the right of the Accies box before picking out Leigh Griffiths in the six-yard area who, completely unmarked, taps in the easiest goal he will ever score to make it 5-0.

35

12 August 1989

Tommy Coyne grabs a second goal in the space of five minutes in the 1989/90 SPL curtain-raiser at Tynecastle. Roy Aitken – who won the penalty that put the Celts ahead on 31 minutes – is set free by a neat pass from Mike Galloway down the right and the Celtic number four's pinpoint low cross into the box is met with a sliding finish from close range by Coyne to make it 2-0 against Hearts.

7 April 2012

Charlie Mulgrew continues his one-man mission to take Celtic to the SPL title. Having scored once, and made another, Mulgrew gallops down the left flank before cutting inside a challenge and then firing a low, curling, right-foot shot into the bottom corner to ensure the Celts head towards the break 3-0 up and on the verge of giving Neil Lennon his first title as manager.

12 March 2017

Stuart Armstrong puts Celtic 1-0 up in the Old Firm clash at Parkhead. Looking for a 23rd successive Scottish Premiership win, the runaway leaders finally break through when a poor clearance by the Rangers defence eventually leads to the ball at Armstrong's feet, and he turns quickly on the edge of the box before firing a low shot into the bottom corner from 20 yards out. It's the Scotland midfielder's 11th of the campaign, though Rangers will end the winning streak with a late equaliser.

36

18 April 1908

The prolific Jimmy Quinn puts Celtic firmly in command of the Scottish Cup Final against St Mirren at Hampden Park. Quinn, who will score 239 goals in 369 games for the club, doubles the lead against the Saints as Celtic chase an historic back-to-back league and cup double.

37

12 December 2002

John Hartson gets the all-important away goal that will take Celtic through the UEFA Cup third round and into the last 16 of the competition. Having won the home tie 1-0, the Spaniards level the scores in the return leg, but the Hoops take command of the tie when Hartson spins on the edge of the box and fires an unstoppable right-foot shot into the bottom corner of the net. Though the Celts will lose 2-1 on the night, the away goal is enough to secure progression to the next phase – the best European run for 23 years, no less.

1 May 2015

A superb team move in which every Celtic player touches the ball at least once ends with Scott Brown tucking the ball past the keeper to put the Bhoys 2-0 up against Dundee. It's Brown's third of the season and it edges the Hoops closer to the win that will all but seal the Scottish Premiership title.

27 November 2016

James Forrest scores in the Scottish League Cup Final for the second year running with a fine individual goal against Aberdeen. With the Hoops already 1-0 up, Forrest picks up the ball just on the edge of the centre circle before powering forward. With no Aberdeen challenge, he is allowed to run to the edge of the box where he fires a low shot past the keeper to make it 2-0 and put Brendan Rodgers's side firmly in the box seat.

38

5 October 1966

Stevie Chalmers books Celtic's spot in the second round of the European Cup. The Bhoys, already 3-0 up on aggregate, effectively kill the tie off when Jinky Johnstone's corner is flicked on by Bobby Lennox to Chalmers, who sees his first shot blocked but reacts quickest to prod home the rebound and put the Hoops 2-0 up in Zurich.

3 May 1986

Celtic's 15,000-strong travelling support go crazy as the Bhoys score another wonderful team goal to go 4-0 up at St Mirren on an incredible day in the SPL. Danny McGrain brings the ball out of defence before it eventually finds Owen Archdeacon who races down the left flank, skips past a challenge and cuts the ball back, where it is dummied by a team-mate and Paul McStay finishes the move with a right-foot shot past Stewart to pile pressure on leaders Hearts who are still drawing 0-0 with Dundee – which would still be enough to win the title, but should there be a slip-up ...

20 February 2008

Celtic go back in front against Barcelona in a thrilling Champions League clash at Parkhead. Lionel Messi had levelled Jan Vennegoor of Hesselink's early header and it is another header that gives the Celts a 2-1 lead. Aiden McGeady cuts in from the left, midway inside the Barca half, before sending a cross towards the run of Barry Robson who connects perfectly to send a looping header just over the despairing fingertips of Víctor Valdés.

15 April 2018

Callum McGregor puts the Bhoys 2-0 up in the Scottish Cup semi-final against Rangers at Hampden Park. Rangers have only themselves to blame as Kieran Tierney dances past a challenge on the left flank before sending the ball into the box, where Russell Martin's poor clearance only finds McGregor who finishes smartly from ten yards to make it 2-0 in the Old Firm clash.

7 November 2019

Mohamed Elyounoussi is the architect as Celtic equalise against Lazio. The Celts know victory in Rome would mean a place in the Europa League round of 32 and when Elyounoussi slides a pass to James Forrest on the right of the box, Forrest controls, nudges the ball on a yard and then fires a thunderous angled right-foot shot into the far corner of the net to make it 1-1 at the Stadio Olimpico.

39

26 May 2001

Celtic edge ahead, looking for a first Scottish Cup Final success for six years against Hibs at Hampden Park. With the Scottish Premier League and Scottish League Cup already secured in Martin O'Neill's first season as manager, the Hoops' hopes of a first domestic treble since 1969 are increased as former Hibs winger Didier Agathe finds Jackie McNamara's incisive run inside the box, and the Scotland right-back guides a low shot into the far corner of the net past Hibs keeper Nick Colgan.

40

8 May 1971

Bobby Lennox puts Celtic ahead just before the break in the second Old Firm Scottish Cup Final in three years. The last meeting had seen the Bhoys go into half-time three goals up, but this is a much tighter affair and the deadlock is broken when Willie Wallace finds Harry Hood, and his clever pass to Lennox sees the Celtic winger move past Alex Miller before planting the ball past Peter McCloy to make it 1-0.

18 February 2006

Maciej Żurawski grabs his second of the game to put the Hoops 4-1 up against Dunfermline Athletic. The Pole times his run behind the defence to perfection as a long ball catches the Pars' cold and he finishes clinically from eight yards with a low right-foot shot into the bottom-right corner.

15 May 2011

Celtic go 2-0 up against Motherwell on the final day of the SPL campaign at Parkhead. Georgios Samaras moves past a challenge and finally plays the ball out to Charlie Mulgrew on the left – Samaras continues his run into the box and Mulgrew picks the Greek striker out and his side-foot finish from ten yards makes it 2-0.

4 May 2019

Needing only a point to secure an eighth successive Scottish Premiership title, Celtic finally open the scoring at Pittodrie. Aberdeen have struck the woodwork and missed a couple of good chances before the breakthrough, which comes when Callum McGregor spots Mikael Lustig's drive towards the box, delivers a superb left-flank cross into his path and Lustig meets the ball with a diving header that gives the Aberdeen keeper no chance.

41

6 November 2010

With Celtic 3-0 up against ten-man Aberdeen, Thomas Rogne hauls down Chris Maguire on the edge of the box, giving the referee no option but to show him a straight red card and level the teams at ten each.

29 April 2018

Odsonne Édouard scores a fine individual goal to put Celtic 2-0 up against Rangers at Parkhead. There is plenty to do as Édouard moves towards the Rangers box, but he drops his shoulder to the right before hitting a low angled shot into the bottom-left corner to edge his side closer to the title.

42

29 April 1967

Jock Stein's magnificent, all-conquering Celtic take on underdogs Aberdeen in the Scottish Cup Final at Hampden Park. Having already secured the League Cup and the Glasgow Cup, Stein's Scottish First Division leaders edge ahead in front of more than 126,000 fans when Bobby Lennox sends in a low cross that Willie Wallace prods home from close range to keep the dream of a grand slam on for the Bhoys.

6 May 1967

Celtic equalise at Ibrox on a day when only a point is required to give Jock Stein back-to-back titles. In dreadful conditions and on a pitch fit for grazing cattle, a shot comes in that squirms loose in the six-yard box and Jinky Johnstone is on hand to prod the ball home from a yard out.

12 November 1969

Celtic double the lead over Benfica in the European Cup second-round first leg at Parkhead. Leading through Tommy Gemmell's second-minute howitzer, the Hoops go 2-0 up as Willie Wallace capitalises on a defensive mix-up to move into the box from the right and hammer a powerful angled shot into the roof of the net.

20 May 1989

Celtic end a poor season on a high with an Old Firm win in the Scottish Cup Final at a sun-drenched and packed Hampden Park. The only goal of the game comes as Rangers full-back Gary Stevens loses concentration as the ball lands at his feet on the edge of his own box, allowing Joe Miller to nip in, steal the ball away and drill a low shot past keeper Chris Woods into the back of the net. The victory for Billy McNeill's side also denies Rangers the treble!

1 December 2013

Celtic wrap up victory before the half-time whistle has even blown against troubled Hearts.

The hosts, forced to field a young side after entering administration, are no match for Neil Lennon's free-scoring side and the fourth of the Scottish Cup fourth-round tie comes after a fine passing move ends with a superb low cross from Mikael Lustig that Joe Ledley turns home from close range to make it 4-0 at Tynecastle.

10 September 2016

Moussa Dembélé scores his second of the game to put Celtic 2-0 up against Rangers at Parkhead. Nir Bitton's precise pass from the halfway line allows Dembélé to race towards goal, followed by Rangers defender Philippe Senderos – as Dembélé gets into the box he cuts back inside before curling the ball past the keeper and into the far corner to send the Hoops fans wild.

43

3 May 1975

Celtic regain the lead against Airdrie in the 1975 Scottish Cup Final. Airdrie have silenced much of Hampden Park with an equaliser, but two minutes before the break, Paul Wilson grabs his second of the game as he heads a pinpoint corner home from five yards out to give the keeper no chance and make it 2-1.

27 April 2003

Celtic take a 2-0 lead in the Old Firm clash at Ibrox that edges the Bhoys towards another SPL title. Didier Agathe is the creator, skipping down the right flank before sending a clever cut-back into the middle for John Hartson to strike a ball that the keeper gets something on – but not enough as Martin O'Neill's side double the advantage just before the break.

19 March 2006

Maciej Żurawski opens the scoring in the 2006 Scottish League Cup Final. With the sad news Jinky Johnstone had passed away just a few days before, the Bhoys were determined to win the trophy for the former Celtic idol. Dunfermline Athletic have held their own in the first half, but as Żurawski breaks in the box, a Dunfermline defender collides with his own keeper and Żurawski picks up the loose ball from a tight angle before teeing himself up and narrowly squeezing the ball home to make it 1-0.

13 September 2006

Shinsuke Nakamura curls a 25-yard free kick over the Manchester United wall and into the right corner of the net without Edwin van der Sar moving to make it 2-2 in a thrilling Champions League group-stage clash at Old Trafford. It will prove a vital goal, too, despite United going on to win the game 3-2, due to Celtic winning the return 1-0 and so having a better head-to-head record with the Reds – which will turn out to be a key stat for qualifying for the round of 16.

44

19 October 1957

Neil Mochan puts Celtic 2-0 up against Rangers in the first Scottish League Cup Final meeting between the Glasgow giants. It is just reward for the Bhoys who, despite starting as underdogs, have given Rangers a first-half thrashing, despite only having one goal to show for all that dominance – until Mochan's strike puts Celtic fans in dreamland at a packed Hampden Park. It is a superb team goal. A sweeping move ends with Mochan collecting the ball on the right, skipping past the Rangers full-back Shearer before cutting in from a tight angle and hammering the ball into the far corner of the net to put the Scottish League Cup Final further out of Rangers' grasp.

26 April 1969

Celtic hit Rangers with a combination of punches right on half-time to double and then triple the lead in the Old Firm Scottish Cup Final. In a brutal encounter between the Glasgow rivals, the Hoops break down the right with Bobby Lennox and after riding a couple of challenges, he finishes with a smart low drive into the bottom-left corner of the net to make it 2-0 at Hampden Park.

1 December 2013

Having just assisted Celtic's fourth against Hearts, Mikael Lustig scores the fifth himself to make it 5-0 at Tynecastle. It's the pick of the bunch so far, too, as the Swedish right-back drives forward, cutting in unchallenged from the right before hitting a superb shot from 20 yards that strikes the underside of the crossbar before bouncing down and up into the roof of the net.

45

26 April 1969

A mistake from Rangers keeper Norrie Martin allows Celtic to all but wrap up a first Scottish Cup Final win over Rangers since 1904. The Gers custodian's short clearance only finds George Connolly, who skips around the keeper before slotting home to make it two goals in two minutes and send the Bhoys into the break 3-0 up and with a real chance of ending that 65-year wait for an Old Firm triumph in Scotland's premier cup competition.

5 April 1969

A simply worked corner results in a goal for Bobby Lennox to give Celtic a healthy 3-0 lead at half-time in the Scottish League Cup Final. Hibs, already with a mountain to climb after a disappointing opening period, are again caught napping as the inspirational Jinky Johnstone spots Lennox's move towards the corner of the six-yard box and floats his corner kick towards the near post, where Lennox casually nods the ball past the keeper to all but seal victory with the second half still to play.

31 October 2001

Celtic take a 2-1 lead over Juventus in the Champions League group-stage clash at Parkhead. Lubo Moravčík has provided the assist for the equaliser against the Italian giants and the Slovakian is again the provider for the second, as his corner is powerfully headed home after a towering leap by Chris Sutton to send Martin O'Neill's side in ahead at the break.

20 March 2003

Celtic take the lead at Anfield in the UEFA Cup quarter-final second leg against Liverpool, predictably dubbed the 'Battle of Britain' by the media. Having drawn the first leg 1-1 at Parkhead and seemingly handing the advantage to the Merseysiders, the Celts need an away goal to have any chance of eliminating Gérard Houllier's team, and on the stroke of half-time, Alan Thompson drills a low free kick to the side of the wall and into the bottom right-hand corner to send the thousands of Celtic fans sprinkled around the ground wild with delight. It also gives the Bhoys a crucial 2-1 aggregate lead on the night.

4 May 2010

Having just seen Rangers equalise at the other end, the Celts retake the lead almost immediately. Lee Naylor whips in a cross from the left and Marc-Antoine Fortuné leaps to head the ball down and through the legs of sub keeper Neil Alexander to make it 2-1 at Parkhead – the score that will win the game and restore some pride with the SPL title already guaranteed to go to Ibrox.

7 April 2012

Celebrations begin as Celtic go 4-0 up against Kilmarnock needing a victory to seal Neil Lennon's first title as manager. Charlie Mulgrew's day gets even better when he picks up a loose ball on the left flank before sending a high cross towards the back post for Gary Hooper to volley home his 21st of the campaign. With two goals and two assists, Mulgrew has virtually sealed the title on his own!

29 April 2018

James Forrest scores a stunning individual goal to put Celtic in dreamland at Parkhead. Knowing victory against Rangers will secure a seventh straight Scottish Premiership title, Brendan Rodgers's men have already scored twice before Forrest's brilliant effort. Dedryck Boyata wins the ball midway inside the Rangers half and plays the ball to Forrest, who jinks past three defenders as he moves into the box on the right and then unleashes a low shot into the far left of the net to send Celtic Park into raptures and ensure the Hoops go into the break 3-0 up.

45+1

6 November 2010

Celtic win a second first-half penalty against a dejected Aberdeen side at Parkhead. Both teams have already been reduced to ten men when Shaun Maloney bursts in on goal and as he takes the ball around keeper Jamie Langfield, the Dons custodian brings Maloney down for a clear foul and an easy decision for the referee. Despite the majority of Parkhead demanding another dismissal, Langfield is merely booked, with Anthony Stokes handing out his own punishment as he just squeezes a shot under Langfield to make it 4-0 at the break.

11 March 2018

Celtic level in first-half added time in a pulsating and crucial Old Firm clash at Ibrox. Rangers, needing to win to keep their hopes of the Scottish Premiership title alive, have twice taken the lead and look to be heading into the break 2-1 up, but as Scott Brown sends a long ball up towards the Rangers box, Moussa Dembélé lets it bounce before cleverly lifting a gentle lob over the keeper to make it 2-2.

45+2

10 December 2009

A superb counter-attack by Celtic doubles the lead against Villarreal in the Champions League. After neatly clearing danger at the back, the Celts work the ball towards the halfway line where Aiden McGeady receives a pass and heads towards goal – he is allowed to run unchallenged until 20 yards out where he hits a precise low drive into the bottom-right corner to make it 2-0.

14 April 2019

Celtic finally break the deadlock in the Scottish Cup semi-final against ten-man Aberdeen. Neil Lennon's men strike in first-half added time as James Forrest spins away from Dons' Max Lowe on the right, before unleashing an unstoppable left-foot shot into the top left-hand corner to give the Bhoys the advantage at the break ... it was a magnificent strike – unstoppable!

45+5

2 December 2018

Ryan Christie scores what will be the winning goal in the Scottish League Cup Final. In a tight game at Hampden Park – and deep into first-half added time – Dedryck Boyata plays a superb 30-yard ball into Christie's path and the striker chests the ball down before firing a right-foot shot that keeper Joe Lewis saves well – but Christie then lashes the loose ball high into the roof of the net with his left foot to give the Hoops a 1-0 lead.

46

16 April 1927

Paddy Connolly – already with two assists to his name – puts daylight between Celtic and East Fife in the 1927 Scottish Cup Final as he races towards goal from kick-off, through the East Fife defence before dinking the ball over the keeper's head and into the far corner of the net to effectively seal a 3-1 win at Hampden Park and give the Hoops a 12th Scottish Cup success in the process.

47

15 April 1970

Playing in front of a colossal Parkhead crowd of 136,505, the European Cup semi-final second leg against Leeds United was a game no Celtic fan wanted to miss. Leading 1-0 from the first leg at Elland Road, the Hoops suffer an early blow when Billy Bremner scores a stunning 14th-minute goal. But two minutes after the restart, Celtic equalise with an excellent set piece. David Hay's short corner to Bertie Auld sees Auld cross in towards the corner of the six-yard box, where John Hughes sends a superb header into the left corner of the Leeds United net, giving keeper Gary Sprake no chance, to make it 1-1.

26 October 1974

Celtic restore a two-goal advantage over Hibs in the Scottish League Cup Final with a superb third of the afternoon. Jinky Johnstone is the creator, drifting in from the left before playing a clever reverse pass into the box that Paul Wilson runs on to and immediately hits a low right-foot shot into the bottom-left corner from eight yards out to make it 3-1 at Hampden Park.

18 March 2001

Celtic end Kilmarnock's resistance to take a 1-0 lead just after the restart of the Scottish League Cup Final. The goal comes via a short corner routine on the right that sees Lubo Moravčík send in a cross that is nodded towards the six-yard box where Henrik Larsson acrobatically volleys home his 45th goal of the campaign.

23 May 2003

Trailing 1-0 to Porto in the UEFA Cup Final, Henrik Larsson equalises for the Celts at the Estadio Olimpico de Sevilla, Seville. Didier Agathe sends in a deep cross from the right that evades the clutches of Porto keeper Baía and Larsson rises superbly to head the ball back across the goal and just inside the far post to make it 1-1. It is a fantastic way for the Super Swede to register his 200th goal for the club.

28 September 2016

Moussa Dembélé – who took just three minutes of the first half to score against Manchester City – takes just two minutes of the second half to put Celtic ahead for a third time in a thrilling Group C Champions League group-stage clash at Parkhead. Pep Guardiola's side will fight back to draw 3-3, but Dembélé controls Kieran Tierney's cross from the left before performing an overhead kick which probably doesn't go in the intended direction but wrong-foots keeper Claudio Bravo to make it 3-2 in a pulsating tie.

29 April 2018

Celtic waste no time picking up where they left off in the first half to go 4-0 up against Rangers. The Hoops, going for the kill after the restart, see a couple of attempts blocked before the ball finds its way back to Tom Rogic on the edge of the box and with the keeper off his line, he expertly curls a 20-yard shot into the top-right corner to all but seal a seventh successive Scottish Premiership title – though the Bhoys aren't quite finished yet ...

48

18 April 1908

Celtic put one hand firmly on the Scottish Cup as Alexander Bennett scores his second of the game just after the restart to make it 3-0 against St Mirren at Hampden Park. The Hoops, chasing a sixth success in the competition, are roared on by the majority of the 55,000+ crowd.

17 April 1933

The scourge of Motherwell FC – Jimmy McGrory – returns to haunt the Lanarkshire men just as he had done in the Scottish Cup Final two years previous. In 1931, McGrory had sparked a recovery from 2-0 down with 82 minutes played to draw 2-2 – and he then scored twice in the replay as the Bhoys beat the Well 4-2. On this occasion, McGrory breaches an otherwise solid Motherwell defence just after the restart to score the only goal of the 1933 Scottish Cup Final and earn Celtic a 14th success in the competition.

5 October 1966

Tommy Gemmell bags his third goal of the tie against Zurich and puts the Hoops 5-0 up on aggregate as he drills home a penalty against the shell-shocked Swiss champions. Gemmell, who has scored 30-yard screamers in both legs, converts from the spot after Neumann fouls Bobby Lennox in the box.

12 April 1980

David Provan doubles Celtic's lead in the Scottish Cup semi-final against Hibs when a dreadful back pass by McNamara is intercepted by the livewire Provan, who skips around the keeper before rolling the ball into the empty net to make it 2-0.

14 May 1983

Losing 2-0 at Ibrox on a day Celtic could win the title, the Bhoys win a dubious penalty just after the restart. Billy McNeill has sent his players out early after the thousands of Celts give a rousing rendition of 'You'll Never Walk Alone' and there is an immediate response. Davie Provan collides with John McClelland as he overruns a burst into the box before making a theatrical fall to the ground. The referee points to the spot, despite the Rangers players' protestations and Charlie Nicholas – in his final game before joining Arsenal – calmly sends the keeper the wrong way to halve the deficit. It is Nicholas's 50th goal of an incredible season.

26 May 2001

Celtic double the lead against Hibs in the Scottish Cup Final. Jackie McNamara has opened the scoring just before the break and the Scotland full-back plays a huge role in making it 2-0, as he bursts into the box before laying a pass off to Henrik Larsson who curls a powerful shot into the top corner from just inside the box.

2 March 2011

Mark Wilson grabs what will be the only goal of a bad-tempered Old Firm clash at Parkhead.

Having drawn the Scottish Cup fifth-round tie 2-2 at Ibrox, the Celts make the most of home advantage as Emilio Izaguirre's cross finds Wilson on the right of the box and his initial shot is blocked on the line by the head of Papac, but the ball falls to Wilson who hits his follow-up into the ground and sees it bounce up and over Allan McGregor and evade Bougherra on the line to send the Hoops fans wild.

3 December 2016

Callum McGregor sparks Celtic into life away to Motherwell. The struggling hosts have gone into the break with a 2-0 lead – this after the Bhoys haven't conceded a goal in more than ten hours of football – but a half-time regroup works wonders when McGregor takes the game by the scruff of the neck, picks the ball up outside the Well box and plays a one-two with Stuart Armstrong before drilling a low shot home from ten yards to halve the deficit.

49

29 April 1967

Willie Wallace grabs his second goal of the game to put Celtic on the way to a 19th Scottish Cup success. The Hoops have edged ahead just before the break through Wallace, and it is more great wing play that sets up the second, with Jimmy Johnstone finding Wallace in the box with a cross from the left and Wallace finishes with a shot into the roof of the net from eight yards out to send three-quarters of the 126,000+ crowd into raptures as the Bhoys maintain their hopes of an unprecedented 'grand slam' of all domestic trophies.

31 October 1956

In the Halloween replay of the Scottish League Cup Final against Partick Thistle, Celtic – yet to win the competition 11 years after it first began – take the lead. After a goalless first match four days earlier, the Bhoys break the deadlock when Billy McPhail intercepts a poor back pass before lifting the ball over Thistle keeper Ledgerwood to make it 1-0 at Hampden Park.

21 November 1998

Parkhead goes wild as Lubo Moravčík scores his second of the game to put Celtic 2-0 up against Rangers. With SPL leaders Rangers reduced to ten men midway through the first half, gaps start to appear in their defence and Stéphane Mahé finds himself in acres of space on the right of the Rangers box, allowing him to pick out Moravčík in the centre who powers a header home from six yards.

10 April 2003

Henrik Larsson levels against Boavista in the UEFA Cup semi-final first leg at Parkhead. The Portuguese side has just stunned the 60,000 crowd with the opening goal three minutes after the break, but Larsson equalises within a minute when Neil Lennon's cross is cushioned down by Stiliyan Petrov for Larsson to drill home from eight yards.

7 April 2011

Charlie Mulgrew opens the scoring for Celtic away to Aberdeen with a somewhat unexpected goal against his former club. The Bhoys have missed a first-half penalty when Anthony Stokes sees his spot kick saved by Jamie Langfield, but the Dons keeper doesn't do as well from 40 yards as Mulgrew floats a curling left-foot free kick towards the six-yard box, but it goes over the head of everyone and takes Langfield by surprise as the ball sneaks in the left-hand post to make it 1-0 in the Scottish Cup semi-final at Hampden Park.

26 March 2014

Celtic double the lead against Partick Thistle on a day when victory will confirm a 45th top-flight title. The goal comes when Stefan Johansen crosses in towards Anthony Stokes who cleverly leaves it, then Kris Commons also lets it run and Liam Henderson collects and hits a low shot into the bottom-left corner for his first senior goal and to put Neil Lennon's men 2-0 up.

26 November 2017

For the third season running, James Forrest scores in the Scottish League Cup Final. On this occasion, Forrest receives the ball on the right of the Motherwell box before shifting back slightly and firing a left-foot shot into the bottom-left corner to make it 1-0 to the Bhoys at Hampden Park.

50

24 April 1954

Alec Young puts through his own goal to give Celtic a 1-0 lead over Aberdeen in the 1954 Scottish Cup Final at Hampden Park. Watched by more than 130,000, Hoops fans would be forgiven if they felt a crumb of kinship with the Dons fans after Aberdeen had thrashed Rangers 6-0 in the semi-final! Neil Mochan attempts from a tight angle but his effort cannons off Dons defender Alec Young and past his own keeper to break the deadlock.

30 November 1966

Bobby Murdoch is the creator as Celtic take a 2-1 lead in the European Cup second-round first-leg tie away to Nantes. His excellent ball allows Bobby Lennox to finish emphatically from close range to put the Hoops firmly in control of the tie on a heavy, muddy pitch.

27 August 2000

One of the greatest Old Firm goals ever? Rangers have clawed their way back into the game after going 3-0 down inside 11 explosive minutes at Parkhead, with Claudio Reyna's header just before the break giving them a lifeline – but Henrik Larsson restores the Bhoys' three-goal advantage with a sublime goal five minutes after the restart. Larsson drives towards the Rangers box before nutmegging the last man and sending a sublime chip over Klos to send Parkhead wild and put Martin O'Neill's side 4-1 up.

15 May 2016

Stuart Armstrong scores a stunning volley to put Celtic 4-0 up against Motherwell on the final day of the 2015/16 season. Mikael Lustig sends in a low cross from the right that Armstrong gently lifts with his first touch before volleying an unstoppable shot into the top-left corner to end the game as a contest. It's a goal thoroughly deserved for Armstrong on the back of a fantastic campaign.

21 May 2017

Leigh Griffiths heads home Patrick Roberts's cross from close range to put the Celts 1-0 up at Parkhead on a historic day for the Bhoys. Crowned champions eight games before, Brendan Rodgers's all-conquering side break through against Hearts in a last-day bid to ensure they become the SPL 'Invincibles' in the process.

23 September 2017

Celtic open the scoring in the Old Firm clash at Ibrox with a superb strike from Tom Rogic. Though the Australian's finish is emphatic, the defending that leads to the opportunity is shambolic as a corner finds its way to Patrick Roberts on the edge of the box – his weak shot somehow finds its way past three Rangers defenders to Rogic who fires a shot into the top-left corner from eight yards out.

51

15 April 1970

Celtic score a second goal in the space of four minutes to turn the European Cup semi-final second leg against Leeds United on its head at Parkhead. Leeds have led 1-0 at the break to make the aggregate score 1-1, but the Bhoys race out of the blocks after the restart to go 2-1 up, as Bobby Murdoch plays a neat one-two with Jinky Johnstone before firing a low drive to the right of sub keeper David Harvey to send the vast majority of the huge 135,505 crowd wild, and with no further scoring, the Celts win 2-1 on the day and 3-1 on aggregate, booking a place in the final against Dutch side Feyenoord.

21 May 1979

In a game Celtic have to win to overtake Rangers and win the title, everything seems to be going wrong for the Hoops. After falling 1-0 down to Rangers – who with two games in hand only need to draw – the Celts are reduced to ten men after a fracas that sees John Doyle and Rangers' Alex MacDonald clash. The referee decides Doyle is the guiltier and sends him for an early bath. Suddenly, the Hoops' SPL dreams look over ...

21 November 1998

Celtic score a second goal in the space of three minutes to make it 3-0 against SPL leaders Rangers at a rocking Parkhead. Simon Donnelly is the creator, bringing the ball forward before threading a pass into the path of Henrik Larsson who shrugs off a challenge before dinking it over keeper Antti Niemi to send the Hoops fans wild.

26 November 2002

Henrik Larsson's 25th goal of the season gives Celtic the edge against Celta Vigo at Parkhead in the UEFA Cup third-round first leg. After a goalless first half, Chris Sutton sees his effort deflected out for a corner, which is whipped in and as Bobo Baldé and John Hartson rise to meet the delivery, the ball falls into the path of Larsson, who shows his natural instinct to nod over the line from about a yard out and score what will be the only goal of the game.

28 March 2004

The Hoops double the lead against Rangers to secure victory and all but seal the SPL title. Zurab Khizanishvili is dispossessed on the edge of the box by Henrik Larsson and the Swede sets up Stephen Pearson who sees his effort saved by Stefan Klos – but the Rangers keeper can't prevent Alan Thompson collecting the loose ball and the Celtic midfielder takes it around Klos before firing the ball home via the foot of defender Bob

Malcolm to make it 2-0. It will be enough to eventually win the game 2-1, move 19 points clear of Rangers in the SPL and extend the Bhoys' unbeaten run to 30 games.

23 April 2017

Celtic double the lead over Rangers in the Scottish Cup semi-final at Hampden Park. Much the better side, the second goal comes six minutes after the restart when Dedryck Boyata foils a Rangers attack and starts a Celtic move upfield. Patrick Roberts moves forward before he plays Leigh Griffiths in in the box where he is brought down by Rangers defender Tavernier. Scott Sinclair steps up to squeeze the penalty past keeper Foderingham's diving hands and then the inside of his right-hand post to make it 2-0 – with the score remaining the same until full time. It is a goal created by a trio of former Manchester City players – Boyata, Sinclair and the on-loan Roberts.

52

24 April 1965

In a thrilling Scottish Cup Final, Celtic level the scores for the second time against Dunfermline Athletic. Having started the second period in determined mood, the Bhoys get the goal their efforts deserve as Bobby Lennox skips down the left flank before sending a low cross into the box where Bertie Auld sweeps home his second of the game with a low shot.

31 October 1956

A second goal in the space of four minutes for Billy McPhail puts Celtic firmly on course for a first-ever Scottish League Cup triumph. Inside-left Charlie Tully plays a superb pass through to Neil Mochan who squares the ball to the unmarked McPhail to fire home his second goal of the game and put the Hoops 2-0 up against Partick Thistle at Hampden Park.

5 March 1980

Celtic take the lead against the mighty Real Madrid in the Hoops' first European Cup quarter-final for six years. Played out in front of a 67,000 sell-out crowd, Madrid fail to prevent Alan Sneddon's raids down the right and the full-back's low shot is spilled by keeper Ramon and George McCluskey is on hand to drill the loose ball home to give his side a narrow first-leg advantage.

29 April 2017

Callum McGregor makes it 3-0 for the Celts at Ibrox on a day that will keep getting worse for Rangers. With the home defence standing off and giving the rampant Hoops forwards too much space, Patrick Roberts nudges a pass left to McGregor who strikes a low shot through James Tavernier's legs to all but end the contest.

15 April 2018

Ross McCrorie's miserable afternoon is ended early as he pulls down Moussa Dembélé to earn a straight red card and concede a penalty in the Scottish Cup semi-final against Rangers at Hampden Park. Dembélé has been a handful for the Rangers defence all afternoon and as the pair chase a ball towards goal, McCrorie tugs Dembélé's shirt in the box and the referee points to the spot. Dembélé steps up to dink the spot kick home nonchalantly as the keeper dives the wrong way to make it 3-0 and keep the domestic back-to-back treble dream firmly on track for Brendan Rodgers's side.

53

19 October 1957

Celtic go 3-0 up against Rangers in the Scottish League Cup Final with yet another superb strike. Rangers have rallied slightly after the restart, but the excellent Billy McPhail's diving header from Bobby Collins's cross puts the Hoops firmly back in command at Hampden Park.

3 May 1975

Celtic get vital breathing space over Airdrie in the 1975 Scottish Cup Final. Bobby Lennox's drive into the box from the left flank is ended with a shove in the back and the referee awards a penalty kick. Paul Wilson – with two goals already in the bag – declines the offer to take the spot kick and regular taker Pat McCluskey steps up to tuck the ball home and secure a 3-1 win in Billy McNeill's final game for the club.

12 April 1980

Johnny Doyle all but books a place in the Scottish Cup Final with a third goal against Hibs. Frank McGarvey's superb cross-field pass finds the advancing Doyle who slides in to knock the ball through the keeper's legs and put the Bhoys 3-0 up.

15 May 2011

Shaun Maloney scores a fine individual goal to put the Bhoys 3-0 up against Motherwell. At a somewhat deflated Celtic Park, news has filtered through that Rangers are cruising to the victory that would secure the SPL title. There is a flat atmosphere initially with the Hoops fans obviously disappointed that 92 points still isn't enough to take the crown, but Maloney knows there is a job still to do and as he drives forward, he drops a shoulder on the edge of the box to create himself a yard of space before driving an angled left-foot shot past the Well keeper to make it 3-0.

26 March 2014

Stefan Johansen virtually guarantees three points for the Hoops – and a 45th title – with the third goal of the evening away to Partick Thistle. The Norwegian wins possession just inside the Partick Thistle half and plays a short pass to Leigh Griffiths who returns the ball into Johansen's overlapping run. He continues into the box before hitting a left-foot drive into the bottom-right corner to make it 3-0.

19 January 2016

Second-half subs James Forrest and Scott Allan combine to put the Celts 6-0 up against Hamilton at Parkhead. The ball is played forward to Forrest who neatly lays it into the path of Allan who immediately nudges it back to Forrest. He takes his time before firing a measured, angled shot across the keeper and into the bottom left of the net.

29 April 2018

Callum McGregor completes the Old Firm title rout as he puts the Celts 5-0 up with 37 minutes still to play at Parkhead. Odsonne Édouard is the architect, cutting in from the left side of the Rangers box before firing a low ball into the six-yard box for McGregor to sweep home and send the Hoops fans wild. Brendan Rodgers's side declare at five and are confirmed champions on the final whistle to complete an unforgettable day for all in green and white.

4 May 2019

Callum McGregor claims his second assist of the game as Celtic edge yet closer still to an eighth Scottish Premiership title on the bounce. Not for the first time this season, it's a set-piece goal involving McGregor and centre-back Jozo Šimunović, who rises above the Aberdeen defenders to meet the midfielder's corner with a towering header into the top-right corner from eight yards out, making it 2-0 at Pittodrie.

54

6 May 1972

Dixie Deans scores from a tight angle to make it 3-1 to Celtic in the Scottish Cup Final. Deans collects the ball on the left of the box and despite the close attention from the keeper and a Hibs defender, he torments the pair as he jinks past them a couple of times each before calmly slotting an angled shot into the net for his second of the afternoon.

3 May 1986

Brian McClair bags his second of the game as Celtic go 5-0 up away to St Mirren. It has been a breathtaking performance by David Hay's side who refuse to give up on their title dream at Love Street. McClair volleys home from close range after good work by Paul McStay, Mo Johnston and Murdo MacLeod to leave thousands of Celtic fans praying Dundee can beat Hearts to swing the title to Parkhead in the most dramatic of SPL finishes. See 83 minutes for more ...

19 January 2016

More horrendous defending by Hamilton allows Leigh Griffiths to complete a 32-minute hat-trick at Parkhead. Accies defender Devlin has time to hack the ball clear but dithers and Griffiths nips in to nick the ball away from him before calmly lobbing the onrushing keeper to make it 7-0 before an hour has even been played in this Scottish Premiership clash.

15 May 2016

Patrick Roberts puts Celtic 5-0 up against Motherwell as the champions turn on the style in the final game of the 2015/16 season. Roberts, on loan from Manchester City, finishes a smart team move as he receives the ball on the edge of the Well box, moves the ball to the left to create a yard of space and then curls a low shot into the bottom-left corner to pile more misery on the visitors – with more than half an hour still to play.

55

4 November 1967

Juan Cárdenas scores a spectacular long-range goal into the top-left corner to claim the World Club Championship for Racing Club. Having won the first leg 1-0 at Hampden Park, Celtic lose the second leg 2-1 in Buenos Aires to mean a play-off in Uruguay – and a game that will become known as the 'Battle of Montevideo'. After two matches littered with sly fouls, spitting, headbutts and violent tackles, the Celtic players are at the end of their tether against the Argentines and the play-off decider erupts into a brawl from start to finish. Four Celts are shown the red card – Jinky Johnstone, Bobby Lennox, Bertie Auld and John Hughes – in a second half that serves only to smear the name of Glasgow Celtic Football Club, with Jock Stein's men losing their rag and sinking to the levels of the Racing players. The 1-0 defeat crowns Racing as world champions, but on the evidence of the three games played, there can't have been a less-deserving team before or since to claim that title.

11 September 1971

Celtic level the scores at Ibrox in a thrilling Old Firm clash. Tommy Callaghan's corner finds the unmarked Billy McNeill who hits a low shot towards goal and

Kenny Dalglish gets the final touch from close range to make it 2-2 – much to the delight of the sizeable Celtic contingent in the 67,000 crowd.

12 August 1989

Tommy Coyne completes his hat-trick to put Celtic 3-0 up against Hearts at Tynecastle. The Hoops clear a Hearts attack and quickly break forward with the ball played to Paul McStay, who cleverly turns with a back-heel just inside the box and Coyne, following up behind, sweeps a low shot into the bottom-left corner to wrap up an opening-day win, though the hosts do pull one back before the final whistle.

2 April 2017

The party starts in earnest at Tynecastle as Celtic edge towards a sixth successive Scottish Premiership title against Hearts. The third goal of the game for the Hoops comes as Kieran Tierney picks out Stuart Armstrong on the edge of the Hearts box and the Scotland international curls a low shot that the keeper can only parry into the bottom-right corner to make it 3-0.

56

22 April 1899

Celtic break the deadlock in the Scottish Cup Final against Rangers, played at Hampden Park. Having just survived a near miss, Celtic break up the opposite end and win a corner. As the flag kick is whipped in, Alex McMahon rises to power a header past Matthew Dickie and into the back of the net to make it 1-0 and give the Hoops the edge in a tight Old Firm battle. The Hoops will add another later in the half through Johnny Hodge – the newspaper reports of the day didn't record the time. The victory, played in front of a crowd estimated to be 25,000, gives Celtic a second Scottish Cup triumph.

7 December 1966

Despite having been 4-1 up on aggregate, Nantes have made it 1-1 on the night and almost taken the lead in a thrilling European Cup second-round second-leg tie at Parkhead. Had they scored another and been within one goal of the Hoops' overall lead, this could have ended differently, so when Stevie Chalmers rose to head home Jinky Johnstone's cross to make it 2-1 and 5-2 overall, there was relief among the 41,000 crowd that the tie was finally put to bed.

31 October 2001

In a thrilling – if ultimately meaningless in terms of Champions League group-stage qualification – clash with Juventus, Celtic retake the lead from the penalty spot. The Italians have struggled with the Hoops' set pieces all evening and as another corner causes confusion, Mark Iuliano is pulled up by referee Gilles Veissière for manhandling Chris Sutton and points to the spot. Henrik Larsson sends Carini the wrong way to make it 3-2 for Martin O'Neill's men.

23 May 2003

In a thrilling UEFA Cup Final at the Estadio Olimpico de Sevilla in Seville, Henrik Larsson again brings Celtic level against José Mourinho's Porto. Larsson, who has scored his 200th Celtic goal just after the break, brings the Hoops level again as he rises to power Alan Thompson's corner from the right past keeper Baía – his 11th UEFA Cup goal of the campaign – to make it 2-2 in a game that fairly fizzed and crackled in the Spanish early-summer heat.

18 February 2006

Shaun Maloney and John Hartson help Maciej Żurawski complete his hat-trick as Celtic go 5-1 up against Dunfermline Athletic at East End Park. Maloney cuts in from the right before playing the ball to the feet of Hartson, who uses his strength to hold off a challenge before playing a pass sideways to the unmarked Żurawski who passes the ball into the net with ease.

57

21 November 1998

Henrik Larsson ends Rangers' brief hopes of getting back in the game with his second goal. SPL leaders Rangers had reduced the deficit to 3-1 a few minutes earlier, but when the ball finds its way to Phil O'Donnell on the left, he sends the ball back into the six-yard box where Larsson powers a header into the bottom corner to make it 4-1 at Parkhead.

7 April 2011

Joe Ledley sweeps home Celtic's second of the afternoon to put the Bhoys 2-0 up against Aberdeen and firmly on course for another Scottish Cup Final. Anthony Stokes is the creator, picking Ledley out on the edge of the box and his left-foot shot goes across the keeper and into the bottom-right corner.

11 March 2018

Jozo Šimunović receives a straight red card from the referee in the Old Firm clash at Ibrox. With the score 2-2 and still more than 30 minutes to play, it looks like a pivotal moment in the Scottish Premiership title race, with Šimunović's flailing elbow catching Morelos and reducing the Bhoys to ten men.

58

8 March 1967

Stevie Chalmers sends the 69,374 Parkhead crowd wild as he puts Celtic 1-0 up against Serbian side Vojvodina in the European Cup quarter-final second leg. The Bhoys had lost the first leg 1-0 to their technically excellent opponents, but Chalmers levels the score at 1-1 on aggregate to set up a grandstand finish with the home support at fever pitch.

5 April 1969

A goal made to look so easy ends Hibs' hopes of winning the Scottish League Cup Final. Bertie Auld moves into the Hibs half before playing a simple pass into the path of Bobby Lennox, who takes one touch before passing the ball past the keeper to make it 4-0. Terrible defending by the Edinburgh side who have been poor for much of the game.

19 March 2000

Tommy Johnson seals victory for Celtic over Aberdeen in the Scottish League Cup Final at Hampden Park. The Bhoys drive forward through the centre and as the ball comes to Mark Viduka, he pushes it into the path of Johnson who drives a low angled shot past Jim Leighton to make it 2-0.

Celtic win the trophy for only the 11th time in 22 attempts!

22 May 2004

Henrik Larsson's fairy tale final competitive game in a Celtic shirt begins. Trailing 1-0 in the Scottish Cup Final to Dunfermline Athletic, a corner is cleared upfield and the Swede collects a long ball, judges the bounce better than the defender, races into the left of the box before expertly curling an angled low shot past the keeper to make it 1-1 – much to the delight of the Celtic fans at Hampden Park.

59

12 April 1967

Willie Wallace has Celtic fans dreaming again as he scores against Dukla Prague to make it 2-1 for the Bhoys in the European Cup semi-final. The Czech side have silenced the 74,406 crowd by levelling on the stroke of half-time but a long ball from Tommy Gemmell catches the visitors' defence flat-footed and Wallace nips in to finish smartly from the corner of the six-yard box – cue pandemonium!

30 November 1997

Celtic go 3-0 up just before the hour mark to all but settle the Scottish League Cup Final at Ibrox. Dundee United have failed to recover from conceding two goals in three minutes midway through the first half and their mammoth task becomes almost impossible as Morten Wieghorst sets Henrik Larsson away down the left flank. The Swede picks out Regi Blinker on the edge of the box and the Dutch winger skips past one challenge, then another, as he drives into the left of the box before crossing in for Craig Burley to power home a header from six yards out. With no further scoring, it means the Hoops take the trophy without having conceded a single goal in the competition this season. It will be Wim Jansen's first trophy as manager, Celtic's tenth success in the League Cup – though a first in 15 years.

11 March 2004

Ten-man Celtic score the only goal of a UEFA Cup first-leg tie with Barcelona at Parkhead. The Catalans have been reduced to nine men after two dismissals, but this doesn't take anything away from what will be a magnificent victory over one of the best teams in Europe. What will be the only goal of the game comes when Stiliyan Petrov sends a deep cross into the box from the right flank and Henrik Larsson hangs in the air to nod down to Alan Thompson, who manages to adjust his body and fire home from close range to send the near-60,000 home fans delirious.

1 December 2013

Kris Commons completes his hat-trick from the penalty spot as Celtic go 6-0 up away to Hearts. Commons hits a shot that is harshly adjudged to strike the arm of a Hearts defender and it is Commons who converts the spot kick, tucking the ball into the bottom-right corner.

15 May 2016

Ryan Christie scores Celtic's sixth goal of the game before an hour has even been played of the Scottish Premiership clash with Motherwell. The referee waves play on after a Celtic player is fouled near the centre circle and Tom Rogic drives towards the Well box – he bides his time before slipping a pass to his left where

Ryan Christie takes over and hits a low shot into the bottom corner to make it 6-0 for Ronny Deila's men at Parkhead.

60

12 March 1892

John Campbell puts Celtic 1-0 up against Queen's Park in the Scottish Cup Final at Ibrox. Despite there being more than an inch of snow on the ground, the referee had deemed the surface playable, but with the gates shut an hour before kick-off, the crowd of more than 40,000 couldn't be suitably controlled and there was spectator encroachment all around the pitch – so much so that the game was voided and classed instead as a friendly, meaning Celtic's 1-0 win meant nothing and a replay was ordered. Played the following month, Celtic win the rearranged final 5-1 to claim a first major trophy.

26 November 2017

Moussa Dembélé scores a penalty in the Scottish League Cup Final for the second season running as Celtic go 2-0 up at Hampden Park. The spot kick is awarded when Scott Sinclair gets in behind the Motherwell defence, only to be scythed down by Cédric Kipré – who is shown a red card after the ref has pointed to the spot. Dembélé steps up and drills the ball down the middle to make it 2-0.

2 September 2018

Olivier Ntcham scores what will be the only goal of the Scottish Premiership Old Firm clash at Parkhead. With Rangers unbeaten under Steven Gerrard and defending doggedly, the Hoops finally open the scoring with a superb counter-attack goal. Tom Rogic breaks forward, finds Odsonne Édouard who in turn passes to James Forrest, and his precise pass across the box is turned home by Ntcham, preserving Brendan Rodgers's unbeaten run against Rangers and giving Gerrard his first loss. It also means Rangers haven't beaten Celtic since 2012.

8 December 2019

Christopher Jullien secures a 1-0 victory for Celtic in the Scottish League Cup Final against Rangers. The game, played at Hampden Park, is settled on the hour after Ryan Christie's free kick from the left flank and Jullien – looking a fraction offside – volleys home with a smart finish to score what will be the final's only goal. It is the Hoops' tenth successive domestic trophy and a fourth League Cup triumph in a row.

61

18 April 1908

David Hamilton ends St Mirren's hopes of an unlikely comeback as he puts Celtic 4-1 up in the Scottish Cup Final at Hampden Park. The Saints have pulled one back eight minutes earlier, but Hamilton's strike just about seals the victory with little more than an hour on the clock.

31 October 1956

Bobby Evans plays in Bobby Collins, who beats Partick Thistle keeper Ledgerwood with a low drive to make it 3-0 in the Scottish League Cup Final at Hampden Park. It is a third goal in the space of 12 minutes and will be the last goal of the game as the Bhoys secure a first triumph in the competition in front of 31,156 fans.

14 May 1983

Celtic equalise against Rangers at Ibrox to make it 2-2 on the final day of the 1982/83 SPL campaign. The Hoops, who know that if they better Dundee United's result, they will win the title, have been two down at the break but a set piece draws Billy McNeill's men level, as a corner is flicked on at the near post and Tom McAdam nods past the keeper from close range.

6 November 2010

Josh Magennis sends a superb header into the top-left corner – unfortunately, it is past his own keeper as ten-man Celtic go 5-0 up against ten-man Aberdeen at Parkhead. Magennis is slightly wrong-footed as Joe Ledley's cross comes in from the right and as he stretches to clear he connects sweetly to bullet the ball into the roof of the net – but not as he has intended!

29 April 2001

Already crowned champions, Martin O'Neill's Celtic look to rub salt in Rangers' wounds at Ibrox. And just past the hour, the breakthrough. Neil Lennon rolls a low free kick to Henrik Larsson on the edge of the box and he holds the ball until laying it into the path of Lubo Moravčík's burst into the box and as the Rangers defence opens up, he slots a low shot past keeper Stefan Klos to make it 1-0 in front of the ecstatic travelling Hoops fans.

21 April 2013

Gary Hooper breaks down Inverness Caledonian Thistle's stubborn resistance to put the champions-elect ahead at Celtic Park. With victory meaning the SPL title will be the Celts' for a 44th time, the visitors dig in and hold out until just past the hour, when Joe Ledley's threaded pass finds Kris Commons who slips Hooper into the box and after a couple of touches, his low shot across the keeper finds the bottom-right corner to make it 1-0.

10 September 2016

Celtic go 3-1 up in the first Old Firm clash in four years. It's a wonderfully crafted goal, with Moussa Dembélé's superb reverse pass putting Scott Sinclair clear and he makes no mistake as he places a low precise shot into the bottom-left corner of the net to give the Hoops vital breathing space in the early-season Scottish Premiership clash at Parkhead.

2 April 2017

Patrick Roberts scores a fine goal to put Celtic 4-0 up against Hearts. The on-loan Manchester City winger runs in behind the Hearts defence as Callum McGregor plays a clever through ball and as another defender takes him on, Roberts sends a rising, angled shot into the top-left corner to put Brendan Rodgers's side firmly in command and on the way to another Scottish Premiership title at Tynecastle.

14 April 2019

Poor defending by Aberdeen gives Celtic the chance to double the lead in the Scottish Cup semi-final. Dons defender Devlin's poor decision to allow a cross to go over his head instead of clearing allows Jonny Hayes to collect the pass and Devlin, in an attempt to make amends, pulls Hayes down in the box. Odsonne Édouard tucks home the spot kick to put the Hoops firmly on course for the final.

62

25 May 1967

In brilliant Lisbon sunshine, Celtic finally level the scores with Inter Milan in the European Cup Final. The Italians have led since the seventh minute and, having won the trophy twice in the past three seasons (losing only to Real Madrid in four seasons of European Cup football), are favourites to win the game, but Celtic have struck the crossbar, seen a goal controversially disallowed and forced the Inter keeper into a number of outstanding saves, until just past the hour when the ball falls to Tommy Gemmell on the edge of the box and the Hoops' left-back thumps a trademark rocket into the bottom-left corner to send one end of the Estádio Nacional into raptures. It was 1-1 and history was beckoning this fantastic Celtic team to go and fulfil their destiny ...

27 August 2000

Celtic again extinguish any hopes of a Rangers comeback with another set-piece goal – the third of the afternoon. Rangers have pulled another goal back to make it 4-2, but a free kick on the right flank gives the Bhoys a chance to again expose the visitors' soft central defensive centre. Bobby Petta whips in a cross with pace and Henrik Larsson soars to glance home his second of the game and put the Celts 5-2 up at Parkhead.

3 October 2007

Celtic skipper Stephen McManus bundles the ball home to put the Bhoys 1-0 up against Champions League holders AC Milan at Parkhead. Paul Hartley's corner finds McManus at the back post and the captain makes sure the ball crosses the line.

25 May 2019

Odsonne Édouard wins and then converts the penalty that keeps Celtic's treble hopes alive. Trailing 1-0 to Hearts in the Scottish Cup Final, Édouard collects a cross into the box and as he nudges it past Hearts keeper Zlámal, he appears to be caught and goes down for a penalty. Replays suggest it was a borderline decision, but Édouard isn't complaining as he tucks a low shot just under Zlámal to make it 1-1 at Hampden Park.

63

15 May 1982

Celtic need only avoid defeat against St Mirren to claim a first back-to-back title since 1974, but the Saints hold out till past the hour mark, leading to anxiety at Parkhead as news that Aberdeen – the only side who can overhaul the Celts if they win by five and the Bhoys lose – are winning 4-0. The goal that settles everyone's nerves comes when Murdo MacLeod combines with Tommy Burns, and it is the latter who plays a first-time pass to George McCluskey who fires a shot into the far right of the net to make it 1-0.

6 November 2010

Gary Hooper completes his hat-trick as the Hoops continue the rout over Aberdeen in the SPL clash at Parkhead. With the Dons in complete disarray at the back, Anthony Stokes spots Hooper's run towards the far post and clips the ball across from the right of the box – Hooper rises above his marker to cleverly head down and into the opposite corner to make it 6-0.

7 April 2011

Anthony Stokes wins Celtic's second penalty of the Scottish Cup semi-final against Aberdeen after being pulled down by Derek Young as he is about to shoot.

Stokes missed the first-half penalty, so Kris Commons takes the duty on and confidently sends the keeper the wrong way to make it 3-0 at Hampden Park and all but seal victory for Neil Lennon's men.

8 December 2019

Jeremie Frimpong's foul on Rangers striker Alfredo Morelos results in a red card for the Celtic defender and a penalty for Rangers in the Old Firm Scottish League Cup Final. The Bhoys, who have taken a 1-0 lead just three minutes before, must face the last half hour with just ten men, but more importantly, Rangers have a chance to level the scores. Morelos takes the spot kick himself, but the excellent Fraser Forster guesses right and saves the Colombian's shot. It turns out to be a crucial moment, with Neil Lennon's ten-man Celtic hanging on to win the trophy for a fourth successive time.

64

24 April 1954

Willie Fernie is the architect as Sean Fallon scores what will be the winning goal of the 1954 Scottish Cup Final. Fernie spots Fallon in space on the edge of the box and the Celtic striker hits a low shot past the keeper and into the back of the net to secure a sweet 16th success for the Bhoys and complete a league and cup double in the process.

28 September 1966

Tommy Gemmell gets Celtic's European Cup adventure up and running with a thunderous shot against FC Zurich. The defender carries the ball into the Swiss side's half before unleashing a 30-yard shot that goes in off the underside of the crossbar to put the Bhoys 1-0 up at Parkhead.

22 March 1972

Celtic grab the goal that will take them through to the European Cup semi-finals. At a tense Parkhead, Celtic – who won the first leg 2-1 against Újpest Dozsa in Hungary – trail 1-0. George Connolly's long punt forward from defence catches the Dozsa defence out and as the ball bounces over a defender, Lou Macari nips in to lob the keeper and make it 1-1. It will be enough to win the tie 3-2 on aggregate.

26 October 1974

In a see-saw Scottish League Cup Final, Celtic score the sixth goal of a thrilling game to take a 4-2 lead over Hibs. It is a superb team goal that does the trick, with the ball eventually played into the feet of Dixie Deans, who – in almost a carbon copy of Paul Wilson's goal some 17 minutes before – hits a low angled drive into the bottom-left corner to restore the Bhoys' two-goal advantage and send two-thirds of Hampden Park wild.

30 September 2001

Leading 1-0 in a vital Old Firm clash at Ibrox, the Celts win a penalty when Lorenzo Amoruso is adjudged to have pulled down Henrik Larsson in the box. Amoruso is shown a straight red – causing the Rangers man to suggest the referee needs glasses – and Larsson steps up to take the spot kick, but Stefan Klos makes up for his earlier howler by guessing right and saving the Swede's effort.

31 October 2001

Chris Sutton scores his second of the game to give Celtic a two-goal cushion over Juventus in a pulsating Champions League group-stage game at Parkhead. Though the Bhoys are effectively playing a 'dead rubber' in that Martin O'Neill's side can't qualify, while the Italians already have, there is still pride to play for and Lubo Moravčík claims his third goal involvement of the evening when his deflected free kick falls to Chris

Sutton, who sends a rocket of a left-foot shot into the top-right corner from ten yards to make it 4-2 in a game Celtic will eventually win 4-3.

27 November 2016

On a historic day for Glasgow Celtic FC, Moussa Dembélé scores to make it 3-0 against Aberdeen in the Scottish League Cup Final. The goal is the result of James Forrest being pulled down in the box by Dons centre-back Anthony O'Connor and Dembélé makes no mistake from the penalty spot to effectively end the game as a contest. The victory is not only Brendan Rodgers's first trophy as manager, it is also Celtic's 100th trophy overall – an incredible achievement.

65

2 April 1923

Appearing in their first Scottish Cup Final in nine years, Celtic edge a tense game at Hampden Park against Hibernian. A fine cross from the left by John McFarlane tempts the Hibs keeper off his line but he is caught in two minds as Joe Cassidy runs in – the keeper flaps at the ball and Cassidy stoops to head the ball into the empty net for what will be the only goal of the game to give Celtic a tenth Scottish Cup success in front of more than 82,000 fans.

12 April 1967

Celtic go 3-1 up against Dukla Prague in the first leg of the European Cup semi-final at Parkhead. With the Czech side conceding a succession of free kicks around the edge of the box, this one is the best placed of them all, on the edge of the penalty area, centrally positioned. Bertie Auld taps the ball to Willie Wallace who thumps a powerful shot past the wall and into the net to give Jock Stein's men breathing space. It will not only be the final goal of this game, but of the overall tie, with Celtic drawing 0-0 in the second leg to reach the final for the first time.

23 September 2017

The Hoops double the lead at Ibrox thanks to a sublime assist by Patrick Roberts. The on-loan winger drifts in from the right before sending a perfectly weighted pass in behind the Rangers defence for Leigh Griffiths, who immediately strikes a low angled shot past the keeper to make it 2-0 and, with no further scoring, extend the Celts' unbeaten run to 57 games in domestic competition.

66

26 October 1974

A goal that will live long in the memory of those at Hampden Park who were lucky enough to witness it in the flesh as Celtic take a 5-2 lead in the Scottish League Cup Final. A deep corner sails over the head of a Hibs defender and lands at the feet of Jinky Johnstone who, slightly off balance, takes a wild shot that looks set to go back out towards the corner flag, but Dixie Deans reacts instantly to head the ball like a rocket into the net. Johnstone shakes his head in embarrassment at such a wild cross – perhaps because it accidentally became a wonderful assist – but Deans isn't complaining as he completes his hat-trick – his second treble in seven days against Hibs who must have been heartily sick of the prolific Hoops striker!

21 May 1979

Roy Aitken turns in Davie Provan's low cross to make it 1-1 in the title decider with Rangers at Parkhead. The Bhoys had been reduced to ten men 15 minutes before, but can't afford to drop a point in this crucial Old Firm clash.

30 October 1982

Celtic level at Parkhead to make it 2-2 with Rangers in a typical blood and thunder Old Firm Scottish Premier

League clash. A throw out by keeper Jim Stewart sees Paul McStay quickly intercept, dance around one challenge and then play the ball off to his left where Frank McGarvey sends a low angled shot from the edge of the box into the bottom-right corner of the net to set up a grandstand last 25 minutes or so.

21 April 2013

Joe Ledley doubles Celtic's lead against Inverness Caledonian Thistle at Parkhead. The Hoops, needing a win to seal a 44th top-flight title, go 2-0 up when Kris Commons finds Ledley who then plays it to the right of the Cally box where Mikael Lustig quickly realises Ledley is now in space at the edge of the box, plays the ball back to him and after controlling the pass, Ledley dispatches into the bottom-left corner.

29 April 2017

Dedryck Boyata puts the Celts 4-0 up at Ibrox as the Hoops head towards a biggest Ibrox win ever. The Belgian defender rises to glance home Leigh Griffiths's free kick from the left as the champions' day keeps getting better.

67

19 October 1957

Celtic put Rangers to the sword again in the Scottish League Cup Final, going 4-1 up as the Bhoys continue to hand out an Old Firm drubbing. The fourth of the afternoon comes when Neil Mochan's corner is volleyed goalwards by Billy McPhail who sees his shot parried by the keeper, but McPhail is first to react, lashing the ball into the net to all but end the game as a contest – only the Hoops are far from finished ...

30 November 1966

Stevie Chalmers scores the goal that puts Celtic firmly in command of the European Cup second-round first-leg tie with Nantes with a second leg at Parkhead still to come. Jinky Johnstone collects a cross-field pass on the right flank before cutting inside and slipping a ball through to Chalmers, who makes no mistake from eight yards to leave the hosts demoralised and well beaten on their own soil.

27 April 2019

On an emotional day at Celtic Park, the Hoops clinch a 1-0 win over Kilmarnock that takes Neil Lennon's side to within a point of the Scottish Premiership title. It is the first game since Lisbon Lions legend Billy McNeill has passed away and how fitting that a player wearing his cherished number five jersey should grab the only goal of the game. It comes midway through the second half as Callum McGregor's corner is powerfully headed home by Jozo Šimunović as the Hoops move to the brink of being crowned champions.

24 October 2019

Ryan Christie levels against Lazio in matchday three of the 2019/20 Europa League at Parkhead. The Italians have taken the lead in the first half and struck the woodwork before Édouard cleverly spots Christie in space in the Lazio box, lays a low pass to his feet and Christie sweeps home a rising left-foot shot from ten yards to level the scores.

3 August 2019

Ryan Christie completes an opening-day hat-trick as the Celts continue to punish St Johnstone. His third goal is the best of the bunch as he takes Mikey Johnston's short pass before unleashing a powerful shot that strikes the underside of the crossbar on its way into the back of the net to make it 4-0 at Parkhead.

68

14 November 2002

Chris Sutton doubles Celtic's lead against Blackburn Rovers to all but seal a place in the next round of the UEFA Cup. Already leading 1-0 at Ewood Park – and 2-0 on aggregate – Stiliyan Petrov sends a corner in from the left and Sutton glances home superbly from the corner of the six-yard box and into the roof of the net to make it 3-0 on aggregate and dump his old club out of Europe.

69

28 September 1966

Celtic score a second in five minutes to secure a 2-0 lead over FC Zurich in the European Cup first-round first leg. Joe McBride picks the ball up just outside the FC Zurich box before nudging the ball left and firing a low drive that takes a deflection off a defender before brushing the inside of the post on its way into the back of the net.

18 October 1967

An estimated 100,000+ pack Hampden Park as Celtic take on Racing Club of Argentina in the World Club Championship first leg. In what will be a violent, disgraceful performance from the South Americans, who do anything and everything to stop the likes of Jinky Johnstone, the Celts stand firm and skipper Billy McNeill soars to head home a corner to score what will be the only goal of a game that will be remembered for all the wrong reasons – though it is nothing compared to the second leg in Buenos Aires ...

7 February 2001

Henrik Larsson wins and then converts the penalty that seals a 3-1 win over Rangers in the Scottish League Cup semi-final at Hampden Park. Chasing a loose ball in the box, Larsson steps on the ball and defender Wilson's

CELTIC MINUTE BY MINUTE

momentum sees him bundle the Swede over for a spot kick. Larsson makes no mistake, sending Klos the wrong way to claim his second of the game and, with no further scoring, win a place in the final.

11 March 2018

Ten-man Celtic go in front for the first time in an epic Old Firm clash at Ibrox. Rangers have twice been pegged back by the Hoops who have then been reduced in number following Jozo Šimunović's dismissal, but as the ball comes to sub Odsonne Édouard, he cuts in on the corner of the Rangers box before curling the ball into the top-right corner for what will be the winning goal of a pulsating Scottish Premiership clash.

14 April 2019

Aberdeen's miserable afternoon continues shortly after being reduced to nine men. Dons midfielder Ferguson dives in recklessly on Tom Rogic and is shown a straight red for his troubles. From the free kick, Mikael Lustig's initial effort strikes the wall, but when the ball lands back at his feet, Lustig has the wherewithal to subtly lay the ball off to Rogic, who fires a precise low shot beyond Lewis into the bottom right of the net to make it 3-0 in the Scottish Cup semi-final at Hampden Park and book a place in the final.

172

70

16 April 1904

Jimmy Quinn completes his hat-trick and scores what will prove to be the winning goal against Rangers in the Scottish Cup Final at Hampden Park. Played in front of a crowd of more than 64,000, this is thought to be the first game where the clash of the Glasgow rivals is referred to as the 'Old Firm'. The first half had finished 2-2 but Quinn's third is enough to give Celtic a fourth Scottish Cup triumph.

12 November 1969

Harry Hood gives Celtic a healthy 3-0 lead over Benfica in the European Cup second-round first leg at Parkhead. To the delight of the near-80,000 crowd, Bobby Murdoch sends in a sweet cross from the right that Hood meets on the full to power a header past the keeper and leave the Portuguese giants clinging on in the competition. It's yet another wonderful European night for the Celts who fully deserve the victory over the side containing the great Eusébio.

20 February 2011

Kris Commons caps a dream home debut with a shot that defies the laws of gravity. Collecting a pass in the middle, Commons drops a shoulder and nudges the ball to his right to gain a yard of space and then strikes a shot with his weaker right foot that takes a crazy swerve and completely wrong-foots Allan McGregor on its way into the back of the net to make it 3-0 and ensure the Celts go eight points clear of Rangers in the Scottish Premiership title race.

3 December 2016

Celtic come from 2-0 down against Motherwell to make it 2-2 and Stuart Armstrong is once again the creator, skipping past a challenge on the left flank before sitting up a cross into the six-yard box that Patrick Roberts heads powerfully down and into the net to make the scores level.

1 October 2020

Odsonne Édouard scores what will be the only goal of the Europa League play-off against FC Sarajevo. It's by no means a classic as Sarajevo keeper Vladan Kovačević spills a fairly routine Ryan Christie shot and Édouard is first to the loose ball and prods home the goal that secures a spot in the group stage of the competition.

71

22 May 2004

The roof of Hampden Park is almost blown off as Henrik Larsson marks his final competitive appearance for the club with his second goal of the Scottish Cup Final. It is the Swede's second goal in 13 minutes and puts the Bhoys 2-1 up against Dunfermline Athletic as he collects Alan Thompson's ball just inside the box, before turning his marker and firing a low, left-foot shot into the bottom right-hand corner. It will be his last goal for Celtic and typical that will it be one that lands a major trophy.

6 November 2010

Joe Ledley scores Celtic's seventh as Aberdeen's afternoon at Parkhead continues to get worse. Ledley's shot from the edge of the box is nothing special, but Anthony Stokes's attempt to connect with it fools the keeper and the ball goes into the bottom corner to make it 7-0.

15 May 2011

Celtic wrap up an excellent season with a fourth goal against Motherwell. The SPL title has gone to Rangers in an epic Old Firm tussle that has gone to the final day, but the Celts still have a job to do and Paddy McCourt wraps up a 4-0 win as Wilson's cross is neatly laid off by Georgios Samaras and McCourt finishes with a low drive from close range. Despite Celtic's 92 points, they are one short of pipping Rangers on this occasion.

1 May 2015

Darnell Fisher is wrestled to the floor by Dundee defender Stephen McGinn to give the referee an easy decision in pointing to the spot. Kris Commons emphatically dispatches the penalty into the bottom-left corner to put the Hoops 3-0 up at Parkhead.

72

24 April 1937

The legendary Jimmy McGrory plays a hand – pardon the pun – in what will prove to be Celtic's winning goal in the 1937 Scottish Cup Final. With the score 1-1 against Aberdeen, McGrory moves forward with the ball and the Dons players shout for handball – but the referee waves away the appeals and McGrory frees up Willie Buchan to slot past the keeper and secure a 2-1 victory – the Hoops' 15th success in the competition.

15 May 1982

Tom McAdam's header downwards goes through a team-mate's legs before being hacked clear by a St Mirren defender off the line – but the well-placed referee adjudges the ball to have crossed the line and Celtic go 2-0 up and edge closer to being confirmed as champions at Parkhead.

9 May 1998

Harald Brattbakk seals victory for the Celts – and the SPL title – as the Bhoys go 2-0 up against St Johnstone at Parkhead. Needing a victory to prevent Rangers winning a tenth championship in a row, Brattbakk finishes a lovely move that skipper Tom Boyd starts from in his own half, scampering down the right before setting Jackie McNamara away and his low cross is stroked home by the Norwegian forward to start the party among the sell-out home crowd who joyously sing 'Cheerio to ten in a row!'

22 May 2008

The final day of the 2007/08 season and one of high drama. Celtic knew a win would bring a third successive title back to Parkhead, going into the game away to Dundee United on level points with Rangers but with a superior goal difference. Rangers were away to Aberdeen and if they bettered the Hoops' result, they would win the title.

The tension at Tannadice was palpable, with only 18 minutes remaining. Then, a corner – Paul Hartley drives a ball into the six-yard box and man-mountain Jan Vennegoor of Hesselink rises in a crowded penalty box to power a header home from six yards. With news filtering through that Rangers were losing 2-0, it was party time for the thousands of Celtic fans in the ground and a third successive title.

3 December 2016

Stuart Armstrong, having assisted two goals already, gets on the scoresheet in a fantastic see-saw battle against Motherwell. The Celts have fought from being 2-0 down to level pegging, then concede again within a minute as Well restore their advantage, but when a pass is squeezed through to Armstrong on the edge of the box, he spins his marker and hits a low shot into the bottom-left corner to make it 3-3 with three goals scored in the space of three manic minutes.

3 August 2019

There is no let-up for St Johnstone as Celtic grab a fifth goal on the opening day of the 2019/20 Scottish Premiership campaign. Olivier Ntcham, on for hat-trick hero Ryan Christie, scores with his first touch, just seconds after coming on. Ntcham overlaps Odsonne Édouard as he approaches the Saints box and Ntcham hits a clever left-foot shot into the top-left corner to put the Bhoys 5-0 up at a buoyant Parkhead.

73

11 April 1925

One of the most famous goals scored in a Scottish Cup final results in this 1925 tie being known as 'the Patsy Gallacher final'. It was an amazing piece of ingenuity by the fan favourite Gallacher who levelled the scores against Dundee with a quite outrageous goal. Trailing 1-0, Gallacher approached the goal and as the keeper came towards him he somersaulted into the net with the ball wedged between his legs. It sent the 75,000+ crowd wild and with the like of the goal never seen before, the bemused referee duly pointed to the centre circle for Dundee to kick off!

28 October 1967

Stevie Chalmers puts Celtic 3-1 up in the Scottish League Cup Final against Dundee United. Chasing a ball towards the United box, Chalmers nips in ahead of the last man before moving past the onrushing keeper and then sending a low angled shot that just evades the desperate attempts by two backtracking defenders and into the net. It is Chalmers's second goal of the game.

5 April 1969

Bobby Lennox completes his hat-trick to pile misery on Hibs in the Scottish League Cup Final and put Celtic

5-0 up in a one-sided game at Hampden Park. A clever through ball sets Stevie Chalmers away and as he bursts forward, he squares a low ball into the six-yard box for Lennox to flick home and score his third goal in 28 minutes.

14 May 1983

Celtic score from another set piece to take the lead against Rangers at Ibrox. The hosts have gone in at the break 2-0 up thanks to two fortuitous deflections but the Celts fight back with a third goal, as Davie Provan's free kick from the right flank is expertly glanced home by Frank McGarvey.

21 April 2013

Gary Hooper brilliantly improvises at the near post to put Celtic 3-0 up against Inverness. The goal is the result of some terrific work on the left of the box by Kris Commons, who skips past a defender with ease before hitting a low cross towards the near post where Hooper flicks home with his left boot after allowing the ball to run through his legs.

74

6 May 1967

Celtic go 2-1 up in the Old Firm clash at Ibrox on a day when a point will secure back-to-back titles. The goal that puts the Bhoys ahead is worthy of winning any title as Jinky Johnstone collects a throw-in on the right before cutting inside past a couple of challenges and unleashing a left-foot shot that arrows into the top-left corner. Though Rangers will level, the draw is enough to retain the title for the Celts who also have a European Cup Final against Inter Milan to look forward to. Quite a season!

6 May 1972

A hat-trick for Celtic striker Dixie Deans as he puts Celtic 4-1 up against Hibs in the Scottish Cup Final.

The prolific forward collects the ball on the left of the box from Callaghan, and as the keeper races off his line he sends a low, angled shot past him with the outside of his right boot to put the game beyond the Edinburgh side.

26 October 1974

More beautiful football by Celtic seals the Scottish League Cup Final against Hibs. The ball is played around the Hibs half before finding the feet of Steve

Murray on the edge of the box, and his measured low shot finds the bottom right of the net to make it 6-2 and ensure the Hoops' run of four successive League Cup final losses is finally ended.

21 May 1979

Ten-man Celtic go 2-1 up against Rangers at Parkhead. The Bhoys come from behind in the SPL title decider when Roy Aitken's mis-hit shot lands at the feet of George McCluskey who controls the ball before turning and lashing a superb, angled shot into the roof of the net from eight yards.

18 March 2001

Henrik Larsson's 46th goal of an incredible season puts Celtic 2-0 up in the Scottish League Cup Final against Kilmarnock. The Super Swede benefits from a lofted ball from Lubo Moravčík to the right of the Killie box and he side-foots a shot that takes a deflection off defender Innes before looping over keeper Gordon Marshall to double the Hoops' lead at Hampden Park.

18 February 2006

Shaun Maloney scores a spectacular volley as the Celts go 6-1 up at East End Park. Maciej Żurawski – who has already completed a hat-trick – spots Maloney on the edge of the Dunfermline box and pings a high cross from the right flank that Maloney watches all the way before connecting acrobatically to send an unstoppable shot into the top-left corner. Fantastic technique.

6 November 2010

Anthony Stokes becomes the second Celtic player to complete his hat-trick as he is gifted the ball by Aberdeen's Chris Maguire just outside the box. Stokes doesn't waste the chance, pushing the ball into the box before clipping it over Dons' keeper Langfield to make it 8-0 in the SPL clash at Parkhead.

29 April 2001

Lubo Moravčík doubles champions Celtic's lead at Ibrox. The Slovakian races down the left flank and into the box before cutting inside of a Rangers defender and drilling a low shot that beats Stefan Klos on his near post to make it 2-0 for Martin O'Neill's side.

5 March 1980

Johnny Doyle doubles Celtic's lead over Real Madrid in the European Cup quarter-final first leg at Celtic Park. The excellent Alan Sneddon has caused the Spaniards problems all evening with his raids down the right and yet again, his overlapping run provides an attacking outlet as Sneddon pushes forward before sending a deep cross towards the six-yard box that Doyle arrives late on to power past Ramon and put the Bhoys in control of the tie and 2-0 up on the night.

75

19 October 1957

Neil Mochan bags his second of the game to put Celtic 5-1 up against Rangers. Mochan and Billy McPhail have tormented the Rangers defence throughout the Scottish League Cup Final and with the Gers' defence all over the place, an unmarked Mochan converts Sammy Wilson's cross to send half of Hampden heading for the exits.

5 April 1969

Hibs' miserable Scottish League Cup Final seems complete when yet more awful defending allows Jim Craig to make it 6-0 to the Bhoys. Craig's run down the right and cross is only partially cleared back to him and the Celtic man opts to fire an angled shot with his left foot instead which beats the keeper and ends the scoring for the Hoops, though Hibs will pull two consolation goals back in the closing minutes to make the score 6-2. News soon filters through that Rangers have lost their league game against Dundee United, effectively sealing the title and two trophies on the same afternoon.

4 May 1988

Celtic equalise in the Scottish Cup Final as Billy McNeill's men stage a dramatic late comeback. Trailing to a 49th-minute Dundee United goal, a brilliant cross by left-back Anton Rogan sails over the keeper's attempt to clear and Frank McAvennie forces the ball home from close range to make it 1-1 at Hampden Park.

1 December 2013

Skipper Scott Brown scores his second of the game to complete the Scottish Cup fourth-round rout against Hearts. The ball falls to Brown on the edge of the box and he strikes a powerful shot goalwards that takes a deflection, wrong-foots the keeper and goes in to complete a 7-0 win at Tynecastle in what is Neil Lennon's 200th game in charge.

15 May 2016

At 16 years and 71 days, Jack Aitchison becomes Celtic's youngest-ever debutant. The teenager can't ask for a more serene situation to make his bow with the Celts already 6-0 up on the final day of the Scottish Premiership season and already crowned champions – but the youngster's day will soon get even better ...

76

26 April 1969

A delightful individual strike from Stevie Connolly wraps up an emphatic 4-0 win over Rangers in the Scottish Cup Final. The Hoops had dominated the game from the off and completed the rout 14 minutes from time when Chalmers expertly chested down a high pass into the Rangers box before turning and firing the ball past keeper Norrie Martin with the outside of his right boot. A superb finish and a wonderful end to this one-sided Old Firm clash at Hampden Park.

15 May 1982

Lovely footwork from Tommy Burns sets up George McCluskey to claim his second of the match and put the Celts 3-0 up against St Mirren at Parkhead. Burns moves past one challenge before splitting two defenders with a precise through ball that McCluskey races on to and drills a low shot past the keeper – the Hoops' third goal in 13 minutes – to secure the points needed to guarantee the title. Aberdeen could have ended up as champions but they needed to win their game with Rangers by five goals and hope the Bhoys got beat by the Saints – neither of which happened.

19 March 2006

Shaun Maloney all but settles the 2006 Scottish League Cup Final at Hampden Park. Awarded a free kick 22 yards from the Dunfermline goal, Maloney steps up to curl a right-foot shot into the bottom-left corner and put the Bhoys 2-0 up at Hampden Park.

21 May 2011

Stephen Craigan deflects Mark Wilson's low shot past his own keeper to put Celtic 2-0 up against Motherwell in the Scottish Cup Final. The Bhoys have been pressing for a second goal when an attack sees the ball played to Wilson on the right of the box and his low drive finds a wafting leg of Craigan to give Celtic breathing space at Hampden Park.

21 May 2017

Stuart Armstrong finishes powerfully from inside the box to seal a 2-0 win over Hearts and ensure Celtic finish a record-breaking season without losing a single game. It's an amazing feat for Brendan Rodgers's side, as they set new Scottish Premiership records for most goals, most wins, most points, fewest losses and the biggest title-winning margin in what is a dream season for everyone connected with the club, dubbed 'The Invincibles' after a genuinely incredible campaign.

77

18 May 1985

Celtic equalise in the 100th Scottish Cup Final against Dundee United who have taken the lead on 55 minutes. After a free kick is awarded on the edge of the United box, Davie Provan shapes up to take a shot, but few could predict the sweetest of goals as Provan curls the ball into the top right-hand corner of the net to make it 1-1 and send most of Hampden Park wild.

1 May 2015

A superb counter-attack sees Celtic go 4-0 up against Dundee in the Scottish Premiership. Nir Bitton starts the move when he wins the ball deep in his own half and then Kris Commons drives forward and with a team-mate either side he picks out James Forrest who runs into the box before dispatching a typically measured low shot into the bottom-left corner.

15 May 2016

Having just become Celtic's youngest-ever debutant, at 16 years and 71 days, Jack Aitchison becomes Celtic's youngest-ever goalscorer barely two minutes after his introduction. In a moment where all the stars align for Aitchison, a ball breaks into his path just inside the Motherwell box and after sizing up the goal, he tucks a low left-foot shot past keeper Connor Ripley and into the bottom-right corner to make it 7-0 for the champions. What a day for the teen and a fine way for manager Ronny Deila to sign off his reign as Hoops boss.

78

7 December 1966

Bobby Lennox completes a 3-1 win over Nantes to book a place in the European Cup quarter-finals. The Bhoys, who have won the first leg in France 3-1, win by the same score at Parkhead as the excellent Jinky Johnstone claims his second assist of the evening as his cross from the right is volleyed home by Lennox to make it 6-2 on aggregate and allow Hoops fans to start dreaming of European glory.

24 April 2003

Celtic snatch a dramatic win against Boavista with a Henrik Larsson goal in the second leg of the UEFA Cup semi-final second leg. Having drawn 1-1 at Parkhead, the Portuguese side look set for a place in the final as the clock ticks towards 90 minutes but when Larsson tries to find strike partner John Hartson, an attempted clearance in the box only plays the ball back to Larsson who drills the loose ball home from eight yards to put Martin O'Neill's side into a first major European final for 33 years.

15 March 2015

Celtic seal a Scottish League Cup Final win against Dundee United – six years to the day since the last success in the competition – as James Forrest makes it 2-0 at Hampden Park. A counter-attack stretches the ten-man Tangerines and after a series of misplaced passes in the box and poor defending, the ball falls to Forrest on the edge of the box and his powerful shot from 18 yards beats the keeper to double the lead and end the contest.

15 April 2018

Celtic finish the Scottish Cup semi-final rout against ten-man Rangers at Hampden Park with the fourth of the afternoon. As the ball comes to Patrick Roberts in front of goal, Jason Holt's attempt at a clearance only serves to bring the on-loan Manchester City winger down and the referee awards the second spot kick of the afternoon. Moussa Dembélé has taken – and scored – the first, but he passes on the duty to Olivier Ntcham on this occasion and he places a low shot in the bottom-left corner to make it 4-0.

Tom Rogic celebrates scoring their second goal against Aberdeen in the Scottish Cup Final (May 2017)

Olivier Ntcham celebrates his goal against Motherwell in the Scottish Cup Final (May 2018)

Odsonne Edouard celebrates scoring Celtic's second goal during the Scottish Cup Final against Hearts at Hampden Park (May 2019)

Kieran Tierney celebrates with his arms outstretched to the Aberdeen fans during the 2018 Scottish League Cup Final

Dundee United versus Celtic. John Guidetti and James Forrest celebrate Forrest's goal in the Scottish League Cup Final (March 2015)

Henrik Larsson celebrates scoring against Rangers with Stephen Pearson during the Tennent's Scottish Cup fifth round match at Celtic Park.

Henrik Larsson celebrates his goal with team-mate John Hartson, against Blackburn Rovers in the UEFA Cup second-round, first-leg match at Celtic Park

John Hughes heads Celtic's equalising goal from a corner, watched by team-mate Jimmy Johnstone and Leeds United's Paul Madeley, Gary Sprake and Terry Cooper (April 1970)

Lou Macari and Bobby Lennox celebrate after scoring the winning goal against Dundee United to go to the European Cup Final, 1970, to the dismay of keeper Ally Donaldson

Georgios Samaras celebrates after scoring his second goal against Falkirk during their Scottish Premier League clash at Celtic Park (August 2008)

Billy McNeill, flanked by two Portuguese police officers, holds the European Cup after the 2-1 win over Inter Milan (May 1967)

Kris Commons celebrates scoring against Rangers in the Scottish League Cup semi-final against Rangers (February 2015)

Scott Brown celebrates with Victor Wanyama who had just scored the winning goal against Hearts in the SPL clash at Celtic Park. (December 2011)

Olivier Ntcham celebrates with team-mates after scoring in the 4-0 Scottish Cup semi-final win over Rangers (April 2018)

Kenny Dalglish in action during the 1-0 Scottish Cup Final win over Rangers (May 1977)

79

28 October 1967

Dundee United are architects of their own downfall with some comical defending in the Scottish Cup Final at Hampden Park. As Celtic attack down the right, two Tangerines defenders collide and the ball falls loose to Bobby Lennox who nips in between the hapless pair and then spins with a low left-foot shot that puts the Bhoys 4-2 up.

80

15 April 1911

Jimmy Quinn finally breaks down Hamilton Academical's stoic resistance by giving the Hoops the lead with just ten minutes of the 1911 Scottish Cup Final remaining. The teams had played out a 0-0 draw at Ibrox a week before and had to return to the home of Rangers for the replay. With time running out and the prospect of a second replay on the cards, club legend Quinn plants the ball home to put Celtic 1-0 up and in sight of yet another Scottish Cup success.

19 October 1957

Beattie's long punt upfield finds the electric Billy McPhail who cleverly flicks the ball over Rangers centre-half Valentine – having a torrid time against the Bhoys' rampant forwards – and watches as McPhail runs past him and on to his own flick before finishing with a smart low drive to make it 6-1, complete his hat-trick and complete a personal triumph in the Scottish League Cup Final – with still ten minutes to go.

12 April 1980

Murdo MacLeod puts Celtic 4-0 up against a woeful Hibs side in the semi-final of the Scottish Cup. The game has become something of a stroll for the Hoops and MacLeod's powerful low drive from the edge of the box gives the scoreline a fair reflection on the match to that point.

26 May 2001

Hibs, looking for a first Scottish Cup final win in 99 years, are put out of their misery as Celtic go 3-0 up at Hampden Park. Hibs defender Gary Smith is penalised by the referee for holding Henrik Larsson in the box and the Swede steps up to drill home his second of the game and ensure the Hoops complete a domestic treble for the first time in 32 years.

26 May 2013

Gary Hooper miskicks at the worst moment to miss the chance of a Scottish Cup Final – but Celtic still end up scoring seconds later. Mikael Lustig's low cross towards Hooper sees the striker somehow fail to connect, but the ball runs to Joe Ledley who collects and hammers a shot into the roof of the net to complete a 3-0 win over Hibs at Hampden Park.

3 August 2019

Celtic score a sixth of the afternoon against St Johnstone. The champions, aiming for a ninth successive Scottish Premiership title, can't have started much better and sub Leigh Griffiths sends Odsonne Édouard clear with a threaded pass and the French striker calmly rounds the keeper before rolling the ball into the empty net.

81

1 September 1888

John O'Connor is believed to have completed a memorable day as he scores his fifth goal of the game to give the Hoops a 5-1 Scottish Cup win over Shettleston at Parkhead. Reports of the game are somewhat ambiguous, but O'Connor was credited with all five goals, yet despite this impressive scoring burst, the 21-year-old would play just twice more in green and white and never scored again. Such was football in the late 19th century.

20 March 2003

John Hartson scores a superb individual goal to put the Celts 2-0 up away to Liverpool at Anfield in the UEFA Cup quarter-final second leg. Hartson collects the ball outside the Reds' box before shifting to his right to open up a yard of space and then firing a ferocious drive into the top-right corner of the net to put the Hoops 3-1 up on aggregate and into the semi-final of the competition.

21 November 2006

Another famous European night at Celtic Park as the Bhoys took on Manchester United, knowing a win would mean a place in the Champions League round of 16. Having beaten Barcelona, Liverpool, Real Madrid,

Juventus, Inter Milan and Benfica on previous glory nights, add the name of Manchester United. After a cagey 80 minutes or so, the Celts are awarded a free kick on the edge of the United box. Shinsuke Nakamura steps up to curl the ball over the wall and into the top-right corner to secure a famous 1-0 win.

18 March 2011

Henrik Larsson bags his 47th goal of the season, completes his hat-trick and seals a 3-0 Scottish League Cup Final win over Kilmarnock at Hampden Park. Collecting a pass on the halfway line, Larsson races towards goal pursued by three Kilmarnock defenders and as he enters the box, he calmly rolls his foot over the ball to round keeper Gordon Marshall before casually passing the ball into the back of the net.

7 August 2016

Scott Sinclair ensures the first Scottish Premiership match under Brendan Rodgers ends in victory as he climbs off the bench to score a late winner in his debut against Hearts. Leigh Griffiths is the creator, skipping down the left flank before putting a fine cross into the middle for Sinclair to turn home and give the Celts a 2-1 win at Tynecastle.

1 March 2020

St Johnstone are denied revenge as Ryan Christie breaks their dogged resistance to give the Celts a 34th successive domestic cup victory. The hosts, beaten

7-0 on the opening day of the Scottish Premiership campaign at Parkhead, are determined opposition with a place in the Scottish Cup semi-finals at stake, but Christie – who scored a treble in the seven-goal rout – is again the Saints' nemesis as he sends in a left-foot free kick that misses everyone and bounces past the keeper for what will be the only goal of the game at McDiarmid Park.

82

11 April 1931

Celtic seem down and out as they trail 2-0 to Motherwell in the Scottish Cup Final at Hampden Park. The Well have scored twice in the first half and are strolling towards victory when Celtic are handed an unexpected lifeline when Jimmy McGrory halves the deficit to restore hope for the majority of the enormous 104,803 crowd.

24 April 1965

Billy McNeill rises high to nod home Charlie Gallacher's corner to seal a dramatic 3-2 Scottish Cup Final win over Dunfermline Athletic at Hampden Park. The Fife side had twice been in front but the Hoops were determined to end their seven-year wait for silverware and a first Scottish Cup success for 11 years. McNeill's goal sends the majority of the 108,000 crowd into raptures.

18 February 2006

Urged to shoot by the travelling Celtic fans after almost five years without a goal, Neil Lennon receives the ball outside the Dunfermline box. He looks for a pass before accepting the invitation to have a go and his daisy-cutter of a shot finds the bottom-left corner to make it 7-1 to the Hoops. A rare goal indeed for Lennon, who would score just three times in the SPL in 214 appearances for the Bhoys.

6 February 2011

Scott Brown scores a superb equaliser to earn the Celts a 2-2 draw with Rangers at Ibrox. In a pulsating Scottish Cup fifth-round tie, Mark Wilson plays the ball back to Brown on the edge of the box and after shifting the ball from right to left foot, Brown sends a curling shot past Allan McGregor and into the left corner of the net to earn a Parkhead replay.

7 November 2012

It's dreamland at Parkhead as Celtic take a 2-0 lead over Barcelona who have twice won the Champions League in the previous four years. For this group-stage clash, Celtic have protected a 21st-minute lead well and when Lionel Messi's free kick is saved by Fraser Forster, the big keeper immediately launches a long ball into the Barcelona half and as Xavi attempts to control it, the ball bounces under his foot and teenager Tony Watts – who has gambled on a mistake – is suddenly through on goal. The 18-year-old is calm and composed as he heads for goal and then hits a low shot past Víctor Valdés to put the Hoops 2-0 up and send Celtic Park into raptures.

25 May 2019

Odsonne Édouard scores the goal that secures Celtic's historic 'treble treble'. Level at 1-1 in the Scottish

Cup Final, Mikael Lustig's powerful header forward turns into the perfect through ball that Édouard races on. The Hearts keeper Zdeněk Zlámal races off his line, the French striker coolly lifts it over and beyond his despairing dive to make it 2-1 and secure victory for Neil Lennon's record-breaking side. A fantastic, unforgettable day for every Celtic supporter.

11 January 2021

Despite having 13 players in isolation due to Covid-19, Celtic's game against Hibernian still goes ahead. Stephen McGinn's foul on David Turnbull results in a free kick on the edge of the box that Turnbull takes himself, firing a superb shot home to put the Bhoys 1-0 up at Celtic Park. Hibs will grab an added-time equaliser but it is still a valiant effort from a makeshift Celtic side.

83

6 May 1972

Full-back Jim Craig plays a huge part in Celtic going 5-1 up in the Scottish Cup Final against Hibs. The Hoops number two skips down the right before playing a neat pass into the box for Lou Macari to sweep home confidently with a rising shot that sends the keeper the wrong way and sends the majority of the 106,102 crowd wild with delight.

3 May 1986

Celtic supporter and Dundee substitute Albert Kidd scores the goal that effectively crowns Celtic champions of the SPL. The Bhoys were winning 5-0 at St Mirren – enough to finish with a better goal difference should leaders Hearts lose – and Kidd's goal at Dens Park changed everything. He would score again in the time that remained to spark wild scenes of celebration at Love Street where the name Albert Kidd was woven into Celtic folklore, even naming 3 May as 'Albert Kidd Day' from that day forward.

24 April 2011

High drama at Ibrox in one of the most crucial Old Firm clashes in recent years. With the score 0-0 and Celtic knowing victory will see Neil Lennon's side go two points clear at the top of the SPL with a game in hand and just five matches to play, Anthony Stokes attempts to go past Steven Davis on the left of the Rangers box but is clearly impeded. In fairness, it looks like obstruction more than a foul but the referee points to the spot. Georgios Samaras places the ball down and keeper Allan McGregor delays the spot kick by asking the referee to move the ball slightly back – which he does – and then Samaras steps up but sees his shot pushed around the post by McGregor to earn Rangers a 0-0 draw. It proves a decisive moment with Rangers eventually winning the title by a point, though the Celts' shock 3-2 loss to Inverness Caledonian Thistle in the games that remained does the lion's share of the damage.

10 September 2016

Moussa Dembélé becomes the first Celtic player for 50 years to score a hat-trick in an Old Firm clash. The 20-year-old – who scored twice in the first half and assisted Scott Sinclair's goal – completes his treble as he collects Mikael Lustig's fine cross on his right foot, before slotting past the keeper with his left to make it 4-1 for Brendan Rodgers's side.

84

22 May 2004

Stiliyan Petrov wraps up victory in the Scottish Cup Final. Celtic, who have trailed 1-0 almost up to the hour mark, have seen Henrik Larsson's double strike put them 2-1 up but Dunfermline's misery is completed when failure to clear a cross into the box sees the ball eventually find the feet of Petrov, who sidesteps his marker before calmly placing the ball in the bottom right-hand corner to make it 3-1 at a celebratory Hampden Park. A fine way to mark Larsson's final match for the Bhoys.

26 May 2007

Jean-Joël Perrier Doumbé grabs a late winner to settle the Scottish Cup Final against Dunfermline Athletic. The Cameroonian stretches to meet a cross from Craig Beattie and gets just enough on the ball to send it past the Pars keeper and ensure Neil Lennon's last game as a player ends with victory, as Gordon Strachan's side complete a league and cup double at Hampden Park.

18 February 2006

Maciej Żurawski completes an 8-1 rout of Dunfermline Athletic at East End Park with his fourth of the game. Stephen McManus sends a 50-yard ball over the top and Żurawski outpaces Pars defender Andy Tod before drilling past the keeper to finish a wonderful afternoon in Fife.

7 April 2011

Shaun Maloney completes a miserable Scottish Cup semi-final for Aberdeen as he completes a 4-0 rout at Hampden Park. The final goal of the game is a fine team effort, as Scott Brown's low cross finds Mark Wilson at the far post and his low cross back across the six-yard box finds Maloney who has the simplest of tasks to roll the ball home from a couple of yards out.

2 April 2017

Scott Sinclair completes his hat-trick at Tynecastle to top off a superb individual performance against Hearts as he strokes home a penalty he won having been brought down by Krystian Nowak to put the Celts 5-0 up. Sinclair confidently thumps the ball to the right of the keeper – who guesses right – but is beaten by the power. It concludes a superb day in Edinburgh as the Hoops go 37 games unbeaten to beat a 100-year club record as well as sealing a 48th Scottish Premiership title – Brendan Rodgers's first as manager.

29 April 2017

Mikael Lustig scores a superb individual goal to complete Celtic's biggest-ever win at Ibrox. The swashbuckling full-back wins the ball just inside the Rangers half before driving towards goal, skipping past a challenge before curling a low shot into the bottom corner from 18 yards to make it 5-1 and create a bit of Old Firm history in the process.

19 May 2019

Mikey Johnston scores his second of the game and the winning goal as Celtic beat Hearts 2-1 at Parkhead. With the title in the bag and the trophy lift to come, Johnston breaks clear before putting the ball past Hearts keeper Bobby Zlámal to ensure the title party can begin in earnest for the near-60,000 crowd.

85

18 April 1908

Peter Somers seals a glorious 5-1 Scottish Cup victory over St Mirren at Hampden Park to give Celtic a first back-to-back domestic double – and the first in Scottish football history. A historic day, but just the first of many incredible achievements by the Hoops – a sixth Scottish Cup triumph.

25 May 1967

The greatest moment in Glasgow Celtic's history as Stevie Chalmers grabs the winning goal of the 1967 European Cup Final. And it is thoroughly deserved against one of Europe's greatest-ever teams, with Celtic recording an incredible 42 shots compared to Inter's five during a superb performance by Jock Stein's all-conquering side. The goal comes as the excellent Tommy Gemmell finds Bobby Murdoch on the edge of the box and his powerful low drive is turned in at close range by Chalmers to send thousands of Celtic fans inside the Estádio Nacional into dreamland. Inter players look spent and are unable to recover in the time that remains, meaning Celtic win the European Cup and become the first British side to lift the trophy. Not only that, it means Stein's wonderful side – later dubbed the Lisbon Lions – have won all five competitions they have entered during this unforgettable 1966/67 campaign. Celtic remain the only Scottish side to win the trophy. Incredible.

8 March 1972

Lou Macari grabs an invaluable late winner to put Celtic 2-1 up in the European Cup quarter-final against Újpest Dozsa in Hungary. The game seems to be heading for a creditable 1-1 draw for Jock Stein's men when two of his bright young stars combine to give the Hoops victory. Kenny Dalglish finds Macari in the box and the diminutive forward swivels and plants a shot past the keeper to put Stein in sight of another major European semi-final.

21 May 1979

Celtic retake the lead in a pulsating Old Firm title decider at Parkhead as the inspirational Roy Aitken again drives the Celts forward before slipping it to his right, where George McCluskey fires a cross in that eventually strikes Rangers defender Colin Jackson and goes into the net to make it 3-2 for the ten-man Hoops.

18 May 1985

Celtic come from behind to score what will be the winning goal in the 100th Scottish Cup Final. The winner comes when Roy Aitken picks up the ball in midfield and gallops down the right before whipping a cross into the box, where Frank McGarvey launches himself to make perfect contact and bullet a header past the keeper to secure a 2-1 win at a raucous Hampden Park.

2 February 2008

Georgios Samaras marks his Celtic debut with a goal against Kilmarnock in the Scottish Cup. The Greek striker, signed from Manchester City on loan, had only been on the pitch 18 minutes after coming on as a sub when he held off the challenge of Simon Ford on the right flank before cutting in and driving a low left-foot drive past the keeper to put the Hoops 5-1 up at Rugby Park.

6 November 2010

Aberdeen's day of misery is complete as they concede goal number nine at Parkhead – a third penalty of the game. Both sides have been reduced to ten men in the first half, but it is Celtic who respond and the Dons who crumble. Shaun Maloney is tripped in the box for the second time and again a spot kick is awarded. Sub Paddy McCourt is given the job of converting from the spot as the Bhoys make it 9-0 in an unforgettable SPL clash.

86

11 April 1925

Jimmy McGrory powers a superb header home to seal a dramatic 2-1 win over Dundee and secure an 11th Scottish Cup triumph for Celtic. Having trailed to Dundee 1-0, two second-half goals settle the tie at Hampden Park with McGrory having the final say after Patsy Gallacher has famously somersaulted an equaliser into the net for the Hoops.

12 April 1980

Tom McAdam shows he has lost none of his striker's instinct as he completes Hibs' misery in the Scottish Cup semi-final. McAdam, who has moved into defence after starting out as a striker, rises highest from a Davie Provan corner to nod past the keeper and make it 5-0 in what is a totally one-sided semi.

14 May 1983

Charlie Nicholas bags his 51st goal of the season and his second penalty of the game to wrap up a 4-2 win over Rangers at Ibrox. As with the first spot-kick award, the second is hotly contested by Rangers – though TV replays would confirm it was the correct decision – as Ally Dawson brings down Murdo MacLeod in the box. Before Nicholas takes the penalty, Rangers fans cheer the news that Dundee United's win over Dundee means the SPL title is going back to Tannadice rather than Parkhead. Nicholas strolls up to squeeze a shot past the keeper to make it 4-2 in what is his final game for the club before signing for Arsenal.

31 March 2019

James Forrest grabs a dramatic late winner to give Celtic a 2-1 Old Firm win at Parkhead. Despite being down to ten men when Alfredo Morelos swings an elbow at skipper Scott Brown, Rangers have levelled after the break and threaten to take what would be a hard-earned point, but a dreadful pass by Rangers' James Tavernier gives possession to Callum McGregor who plays it to Édouard. The French striker holds the ball moves away from a challenge before spotting Forrest's burst into the box. The Celts winger takes one touch before firing a low shot past the keeper to win the game and put the Hoops 13 points clear of Rangers with just six games remaining.

3 August 2019

Leigh Griffiths completes the opening day rout of St Johnstone with the seventh goal of an impressive display. Griffiths, who has already assisted one goal since coming on as sub, matches the feat of Olivier Ntcham who has also scored after coming on as sub, as he collects Ntcham's pass on the edge of the box before striking a low left-foot shot into the bottom-right corner from 20 yards to make it 7-0.

87

6 May 1972

Lou Macari wraps up the biggest Scottish Cup Final win since 1888 as Celtic complete a 6-1 thrashing of Hibernian. Yet again, right-back Jim Craig – creator of the fifth goal – races clear down the right flank before his low cross is half cleared off the line by a Hibs defender, but only as far as George Connolly who sends the ball back into the six-yard box for Macari to prod home his second in four minutes and complete the rout of the Edinburgh men.

30 October 1982

Murdo MacLeod settles a wonderful Old Firm clash with a winner three minutes from time. Celtic had twice been behind to Rangers in the Scottish Premier League clash at Parkhead but had fought back each time to level the scores. Then, with both teams having given their all on a miserable autumnal Glasgow evening, Charlie Nicholas turns his marker and plays a pass to the overlapping MacLeod. He takes the ball in his stride before hitting a low angled shot into the bottom-right corner from the edge of the box to seal a 3-2 victory and send the majority of the 60,408 crowd wild.

29 April 2001

Henrik Larsson scores the 50th goal of an incredible season for the Swedish striker. Already leading 2-0 at Ibrox and previously crowned champions, the Bhoys put the icing on the cake with a third goal three minutes from the end. Martin O'Neill's team have rarely threatened the Rangers goal until Moravčík puts them ahead in the 61st minute. Jackie McNamara dispossesses Tugay on the left flank before supplying an incisive pass to the Swedish goal machine, who takes the ball past Klos and then rolls home from a seemingly impossible angle to make it 3-0.

88

15 April 1931

Jimmy McGrory's second goal of the game seals a 13th Scottish Cup triumph for Celtic. Motherwell have fought their way back into the game following George Stevenson's goal midway through the second period, but after yet another howler by Well keeper McClory, Hoops striker McGrory kills the game two minutes from time to secure a 4-2 replay win at Hampden Park.

28 October 1967

Celtic finally kill off the challenge of Dundee United in a hugely entertaining Scottish League Cup Final at Hampden Park. It is the fifth goal in 15 minutes of an eight-goal thriller, with the Tangerines repeatedly fighting back when all seems lost. A long punt forward splits the United defence and bounces kindly as Stevie Chalmers nods it almost out of the keeper's hands. Willie Wallace – alongside his team-mate – is on hand to roll the ball into the empty net to make it 5-3 and deny Chalmers his hat-trick. It is the first time any club has won the Scottish League Cup final three times in succession.

21 May 2011

Charlie Mulgrew completes a 3-0 Scottish Cup Final victory over Motherwell with a stunning free kick. It is the icing on the cake at a rain-soaked Hampden Park, with Mulgrew firing a missile of a shot through the defensive wall and into the top-left corner to give keeper Darren Randolph no chance and secure a first trophy for Neil Lennon in his debut season as the Hoops manager.

7 April 2012

Joe Ledley dinks home Celtic's fifth of the afternoon against Kilmarnock. Ledley runs into the box after a fine team move of fast, incisive football and as the keeper races off his line, the skipper calmly lifts it over and into the net to put the Hoops 5-0 up at Rugby Park.

1 May 2015

Nir Bitton completes a fine individual display with a superb goal to put the Celts 5-0 up against Dundee in what will prove to be a title-winning performance. Bitton, heavily involved in two of Celtic's goals, receives a pass halfway inside the Dundee half and from fully 35 yards he hits a shot that flies like an arrow into the top-right corner of the net. The win leaves the Hoops 11 points clear of Aberdeen, who lose their game 1-0 at Dundee United a day later to mean Celtic cannot be caught and they are handed the title without actually playing.

4 May 2019

Party time at Pittodrie as Celtic seal the three points that ensure they are Scottish Premiership champions for the eighth time in a row. Édouard claims his 21st goal of the season when he receives the ball on the edge of the Aberdeen box before striking a low shot through the legs of an Aberdeen defender and into the bottom-left corner to make it 3-0 at Pittodrie.

89

11 April 1931

Celtic complete a remarkable comeback to salvage a draw and force a Scottish Cup Final replay. The Hoops have trailed to two first-half Motherwell goals at Hampden Park, but after pulling one back on 82 minutes, the Well shoot themselves in the foot in the last minute, as defender Allan Craig's attempted header back to keeper Alan McClory goes into his own net to make it 2-2 and earn Celtic another crack at the trophy they've already won 12 times.

7 May 1966

Bobby Lennox's dramatic last-minute goal secures a first league title for Celtic in 12 years and also gives Jock Stein his first championship at the start of a fantastic era for the Bhoys, who will go on to win eight Division One titles in a row.

Knowing that victory would mean being crowned champions on points rather than ending on the same points but a superior goal difference to Rangers, Celtic look like settling for a 0-0 draw with Motherwell at Fir Park, but one last raid down the right does the trick as Jinky Johnstone feeds the overlapping Jim Craig with a threaded pass inside the full-back and from the byline, the right-back crosses low into the six-yard box and

Bobby Lennox bundles the ball over the line to secure a 1-0 win.

4 May 1974

Celtic finally seal victory over a Dundee United side who have made the Hoops fight all the way. The third goal of the game comes as a long ball up front finds Kenny Dalglish in space in the United half – Dalglish lets the ball run on and then hooks a pass to his left where Dixie Deans controls and then casually curls a shot past three defenders and into the bottom-right corner of the net to make it 3-0 and secure yet another Scottish Cup triumph and a fifth league and cup double in eight years.

21 November 1998

Mark Burchill completes a fantastic afternoon for Celtic fans as he scores the final goal of a 5-1 hammering of Rangers at Parkhead. The SPL leaders are humbled as Henrik Larsson moves forward and threads an angled pass into the path of second-half sub Mark Burchill, who hits a first-time left-foot shot across the keeper and into the bottom-right corner to seal an emphatic Old Firm victory for the Bhoys.

21 November 2006

With the vast majority of Celtic Park urging the referee to blow his whistle, Manchester United win a free kick on the edge of the Hoops' box. Cristiano Ronaldo steps up and fires his free kick into the wall, but the referee spots

Shaun Maloney has used his arm to deflect the ball away and so awards a penalty. Louis Saha steps up to take the spot kick but his low shot to the left is brilliantly saved by Artur Boruc – cue frenzied celebrations around the ground with the final whistle shortly after confirming Champions League round of 16 qualification for the first time.

21 April 2013

Georgios Samaras scores a fine individual goal as Celtic go 4-0 up against Inverness to wrap up a 44th top-flight title. The Greek striker carries the ball into the left of the Cally box before jinking one way, then the other, to get the ball on his left foot before firing a thumping angled shot in off the underside of the bar to cap a wonderful day at Parkhead.

19 January 2016

Hamilton's rearguard action is finally broken – the fact the Accies haven't conceded another goal since falling 7-0 down some 35 minutes earlier is a miracle in itself, but any hopes of having at least shored up somewhat in the final third of the game – and even pulled a decent goal back – are ended by Celtic's eighth of the game a minute from time as Callum McGregor hits a powerful low drive into the bottom-right corner from the edge of the box to seal an 8-1 rout.

The Hoops' biggest win since beating Aberdeen 9-0 in 2010.

24 October 2019

Christopher Jullien's header gives Celtic a 2-1 Europa League group-stage win over Lazio at Parkhead. In an entertaining game, Neil Lennon's side have fought from 1-0 down to level through Ryan Christie, and it is from Christie's corner that Jullien soars to power a header past Lazio keeper Strakosha to seal a dramatic late 2-1 win for the Bhoys.

90

15 April 1911

Thomas McAteer seals a seventh Scottish Cup success for Celtic by putting the Bhoys 2-0 up against Hamilton Academical at Ibrox. The two sides had played out more than three hours of goalless football in the final having drawn the first meeting 0-0 – but Jimmy Quinn's 80th-minute goal meant the Accies had to take more chances and McAteer slotted home to guarantee the trophy headed back to Parkhead.

19 October 1957

The scourge of Rangers is again at the heart of the move that leads to a humiliating seventh Celtic goal in the Scottish League Cup Final. Billy McPhail – already a hat-trick hero – is pulled down in the box and Willie Fernie converts the resulting penalty to make it 7-1 and spark violent scenes in the Rangers section of the 82,000+ Hampden Park crowd.

8 March 1967

They still call it the loudest roar ever heard at Parkhead as Celtic finally got the second goal that booked a place in the European Cup semi-finals. With the score on the night 1-0 to the Bhoys, but 1-1 on aggregate against Serbian side Vojvodina, Celtic win a corner in the final minute of the game. Charlie Gallagher runs over to take it, roared on by almost 70,000 fans in green and white, and as the ball swings across, who else but skipper Billy McNeill soars to head it home and send Parkhead wild. The 2-0 scoreline means a 2-1 aggregate success and there is just enough time for Vojvodina to kick the ball for the restart before the referee blows for full time, sparking scenes of joy on and off the pitch and booking a semi-final berth for Jock Stein's wonderfully talented side.

11 September 1971

A goal created by a diminutive trio of Celtic forwards gives the Bhoys a dramatic last-minute Old Firm winner at Ibrox. With the game seemingly heading for a draw, Lou Macari lifts the ball to Kenny Dalglish on the left of the Rangers box and his chip into the middle finds the head of Jinky Johnstone, who leaps high to loop a header over the keeper and a clutch of defenders on the line to make it 3-2 and settle the game.

21 May 1979

The exhausted ten men of Celtic launch one final attack against Rangers. Leading 3-2 but knowing a Rangers goal would end the Hoops' title hopes, Murdo MacLeod comes forward for one last foray and as he gets to the left of the Rangers box, he unleashes a superb shot from 20 yards that fairly flies into the roof of the net to make it 4-2 and ensure the Celts are SPL champions and end Rangers' chances. It also gives club legend Billy

McNeill his first title as manager following Jock Stein's departure from Parkhead.

14 May 1988

Frank McAvennie snatches victory from the jaws of defeat with a last-gasp Scottish Cup Final winner against Dundee United. The Tangerines have led 1-0 up to the 75th minute but two goals from McAvennie ensure the Bhoys' centenary season ends with a league and cup double. Billy Stark's deflected shot lands at the feet of McAvennie, who bundles the ball over the line to send 70,000 Celtic fans wild. A wonderful end to a wonderful season for Billy McNeill's men.

27 August 2000

Chris Sutton scores his second goal in his first Old Firm match to complete 'the demolition derby' at Parkhead. Rangers have been unable to deal with set pieces – or strikers Henrik Larsson and Sutton – on a miserable afternoon for the champions, and Stéphane Mahé's low cross from the left finds Sutton in the six-yard box and he makes no mistake from a couple of yards to complete a 6-2 rout for Martin O'Neill's side – and the dawn of a new era for the Hoops.

30 September 2001

Celtic wrap up three points at Ibrox to settle the SPL Old Firm clash with a last-minute goal – and what a goal it is. Alan Thompson picks the ball up on the left flank with two Rangers players around him. A quick drop of the shoulder and burst of pace sees Thompson break free and as another challenge comes in he drifts past with ease into the box before tucking a low shot past Stefan Klos into the bottom-right corner to make it 2-0 and send the Bhoys seven points clear at the top of the table.

3 October 2007

Celtic snatch a late win over AC Milan who are defending their Champions League title won the previous May. With the sides tied at 1-1, a draw would be a creditable result for the Celts, but when Gary Caldwell's shot is only parried by Milan keeper Dida, Scott McDonald tucks the loose ball away to secure three group-stage points against the Italians.

7 April 2012

Gary Hooper seals a fantastic 6-0 victory as Celtic are crowned champions against Kilmarnock. Anthony Stokes's attempt to pass a Killie defender on the right sees the ball break to Hooper outside the box and he controls with his left foot before firing a thunderous shot into the top-right corner to complete the rout and bring the SPL title back to Parkhead for the first time in four years.

2 October 2012

Georgios Samaras scores the winner in Moscow for the second time in three years. The Greek striker had bagged a dramatic winner against the same opponents in 2009 after coming on as sub and this time he gets the Bhoys' Champions League group-stage campaign off to a flyer, leaping like a salmon to head home Emilio Izaguirre's fine cross and secure a historic first group-stage away victory.

3 December 2016

Tom Rogic scores a dramatic winner against Motherwell to secure a 4-3 win at Fir Park. The Hoops had been 2-0 down and 3-2 down but fought back each time, so it was fitting the first time Brendan Rodgers's side should take the lead was in the dying seconds. With one of the last attacks of the game, James Forrest plays a short pass to Rogic on the edge of the box and the Australian cuts in from the left before hitting a low angled shot from the edge of the box and into the bottom-right corner to secure a 4-3 win.

24 September 2020

A sweeping move that starts with keeper Vasilis Barkas results in Celtic scoring a last-minute winner against Latvian champions Riga in the one-legged Europa League third qualifying round. Ryan Christie feeds Jeremie Frimpong on the right and his cross finds substitute Mohamed Elyounoussi who hits a low shot home for his third goal of the season. In the revised format of the competition due to the pandemic and travel restrictions, the goal ensures Celtic don't have to play another 30 minutes of extra time or even the prospect of the dreaded penalty shoot-out.

4 October 2020

Leigh Griffiths finally breaks St Johnstone's stubborn resistance with a powerful header to put the Celts 1-0 up to maintain Neil Lennon's side's unbeaten start to 2020/21. Hatem Elhamed receives a short pass on the right flank and his excellent cross allows Griffiths to power a header into the bottom-right corner in the behind-closed-doors clash in Perth.

Added time ...

90+1

22 April 2007

Shinsuke Nakamura wins and then scores from the free kick that seals the SPL title against Kilmarnock. With the score 1-1 going into added time, Gary Wales shoves Shinsuke in the back, just to the right, outside the Killie box. With the Celtic fans behind the goal baying for a winner, Nakamura steps back and then curls a left-foot shot over and around the wall and into the left corner for the winning goal as the majority of Rugby Park goes wild. Champions again!

5 August 2009

Georgios Samaras climbs off the bench to score a dramatic winner against Spartak Moscow. Celtic had lost the first leg in Glasgow 1-0 but led in the return game through a Scott McDonald header. Samaras's winner comes in added time as he weaves across the box before squeezing a low shot inside the post to give Tony Mowbray's side a 2-0 victory and give the Bhoys a first win away in Europe for 23 matches, not to mention overturning a first-leg defeat for the first time.

90+2

19 March 2006

Substitute Dion Dublin gets his first Celtic goal to put the icing on the cake in the Scottish League Cup Final. With seconds remaining, Dublin, who has come on for the injured Roy Keane, finishes with a clever flick from a low cross in from the right to seal a 3-0 win over Dunfermline Athletic. It is Gordon Strachan's first trophy as Celtic manager in a game dedicated to the memory of the recently passed Celtic legend Jinky Johnstone.

28 August 2013

James Forrest completes a memorable comeback for Celtic against Shakhter Karagandy at Parkhead. Having lost 2-0 to the Kazakhstanis in the first leg, the Bhoys fight back to level the aggregate scores as extra time beckons. Then, in one last surge forward, Anthony Stokes weaves his way into the box and then pulls the ball back for Forrest, who thumps home a shot to make it 3-0 and send Celtic through to the Champions League group stage.

26 March 2014

Anthony Stokes gets the title party really going as he puts the Celts 4-1 up away to Partick Thistle. Georgios

Samaras wriggles away from a challenge before playing the ball to Stokes on the edge of the box. Stokes tees up the ball before striking a beauty into the top right-hand corner from 15 yards to wrap up a third successive championship for Neil Lennon's all-conquering side.

10 September 2016

Stuart Armstrong completes an Old Firm rout over Rangers as he makes it 5-1 at Parkhead. Kieran Tierney beats his man on the left of the Rangers box before cleverly picking out Armstrong with a low cross into the middle – Armstrong controls the pass before drilling the ball into the bottom-left corner. The victory maintains Celtic's 100 per cent Scottish Premiership record with four games played and opens up a four-point gap on Rangers who have also played one game more.

27 May 2017

Celtic end an extraordinary season in perfect style with a last-gasp winner to secure the Scottish Cup and complete an unprecedented unbeaten domestic treble at Hampden Park. Aberdeen had more than played their part in a thrilling final, but the Dons – looking for a first final triumph in 27 years – were tiring rapidly and as Tom Rogic launched one final attack, he perhaps sensed he had the legs the defenders in front of him didn't. He collects the ball midway in the Aberdeen half before bursting past one defender and into the box where he teases his marker and then nudges the ball to the right, before beating the keeper with a crisp low shot at the near post to send the Celtic fans wild and confirm the Hoops' undisputed title as kings of Scottish football after an incredible 2016/17 season.

90+3

16 April 2008

Has Parkhead ever been noisier? True, there are many games to choose from, but to win a game that you cannot afford to lose – and it to be against Rangers – deep into added time must be right up there with the best moments. With Rangers four points ahead and just five games remaining, the Celts throw one last attack as Gary Caldwell dinks the ball towards the corner of the six-yard box, Scott McDonald heads it back into the middle and the towering Jan Vennegoor of Hesselink nods past Allan McGregor from close range to seal a crucial 2-1 win.

26 March 2014

The icing on the cake at Fir Park as Celtic are confirmed inaugural winners of the newly named Scottish Premiership with a thumping win against Partick Thistle. Georgios Samaras's cameo off the subs' bench continues with his second assist of the game, this time driving towards goal before laying to his right where Kris Commons strikes a ball through the keeper to complete a 5-1 win.

19 February 2015

John Guidetti, a 75th-minute sub, grabs a dramatic last-gasp leveller as Celtic make it 3-3 in an absorbing

Europa League round of 32 first-leg tie at Parkhead. Having twice been behind, it's vital Ronny Deila's side go to Italy with something to cling on to, and Guidetti supplies a lifeline as he chests down Liam Henderson's chipped pass into the box before sending a fierce half-volley into the top-left corner to make it 3-3.

1 September 2019

Celtic seal victory over Steven Gerrard's Rangers to move three points clear at the top of the Scottish Premiership. Odsonne Édouard and Olivier Ntcham combine to put sub Jonny Hayes clear and though keeper McGregor saves his initial shot, Hayes is on hand to gather the loose ball, take it past a defender and then hammer home to make it 2-0 deep into added time at Ibrox.

4 October 2020

After waiting 90 minutes to break down a resolute St Johnstone defence, the Celts score a second goal in the space of three minutes to wrap up three points and move above Rangers in the Scottish Premiership table. The basement Saints drop their concentration after Leigh Griffiths's opener and Patryk Klimala rides a challenge in the box before finishing powerfully from close range to make it 2-0.

90+4

16 March 2013

Celtic complete a remarkable comeback at Parkhead to beat Aberdeen 4-3. Despite having been in front after just 13 seconds, the Bhoys slump to 3-1 down against the Dons before rallying back to 3-3 in a thrilling SPL encounter – then, enter super-sub Georgios Samaras. As a free kick is nodded back to the edge of the six-yard box – back to goal – the Greek striker cleverly strikes an overhead kick past the keeper for an injury-time winner.

90+5

7 November 2019

Olivier Ntcham secures a historic 2-1 win for Celtic, deep into stoppage time at the Stadio Olimpico in Rome. Drawing 1-1 with Lazio, Édouard intercepts a poor pass out of defence and drives towards goal before playing it to the unmarked Ntcham who looks to have gone slightly too wide as the keeper approaches, but the former Manchester City man gently dinks the ball over the diving Strakosha to win the game for Neil Lennon's men and send 10,000 or so Celtic fans wild. It is the Celts' first-ever win on Italian soil.

Extra time

91

15 March 2009

Celtic take the lead in the first minute of extra time in the 2009 Scottish League Cup Final against Rangers. Awarded a free kick on the left of the Rangers box, Shinsuke Nakamura swings a cross into the six-yard box where Darren O'Dea rises to head powerfully past Allan McGregor to break the deadlock and put the Hoops 1-0 up.

94

23 May 2003

A massive blow as Celtic are reduced to ten men four minutes into extra time in the UEFA Cup Final against José Mourinho's Porto as Bobo Baldé is sent off for a second bookable offence following a reckless challenge on Derlei. Baldé's dismissal severely dents the Bhoys' hopes of a first European trophy for 36 years – and when Porto grab the winner five minutes from the end of extra time, Martin O'Neill's side can't find a third equaliser to force penalties. A brave performance but ultimately one that goes unrewarded.

98

7 November 2006

Celtic finally break the deadlock in the Scottish League Cup clash with Falkirk. The Bhoys, defending the trophy, find it hard to break down Falkirk in 90 minutes with the scores level at 0-0. But when Maciej Żurawski heads Jan Vennegoor of Hesselink's cross in eight minutes into extra time, it looks like Gordon Strachan's side will go on to win the game. Falkirk, however, have other ideas and will level a minute later and then win 5-4 on penalties.

103

19 April 2015

Swedish striker John Guidetti keeps hopes of a domestic treble alive in the Scottish Cup semi-final as he pulls the Hoops level with Inverness at Hampden Park. Scott Brown's driving run towards goal is thwarted by two Cally players combining to block the skipper's path. Guidetti steps up and his free kick looks to lack pace as it goes over the wall, but the keeper misjudges the shot and lets it bounce over him and into the corner of the net to make it 2-2. Inverness will strike again three minutes from time to claim their first-ever appearance in the final.

105

20 December 2020

Hearts, having been relegated in the interim coronavirus-affected 2019/20 season, had fought back from 2-0 down to draw 2-2 in normal time with Celtic in the much delayed Scottish Cup Final at Hampden Park. But in extra time, it is the holders who edge ahead again as Ryan Christie's corner is powerfully headed goalwards by Scott Brown, but after a fine save from the keeper, sub Leigh Griffiths reacts quickest to fire a shot into the roof of the net to make it 3-2 – though the Jambos will level before extra time is completed to force penalties at Hampden Park.

107

10 May 1980

Celtic score what will prove to be an extra-time winning goal to settle the Old Firm Scottish Cup Final at Hampden Park. The match has ended normal time with the scores level at 0-0, but as a cross into the Rangers box is headed clear, skipper Danny McGrain sends a low volley goalwards from outside the box and George McCluskey's deft touch sends the goalkeeper the wrong way and the ball into the back of the net. The victory is followed by a pitch invasion from both sets of fans, resulting in what later became known as the 'Hampden Park Riot' – and an alcohol ban at Scottish football matches that remains in place to this day.

114

17 August 2019

James Forrest grabs the winning goal in a hard-fought Scottish League Cup win over Championship side Dunfermline Athletic. The Pars have defended doggedly throughout, holding the Hoops to 1-1 in normal time and looking set to force a penalty shoot-out to decide the winners at Celtic Park, until Forrest's deflected shot beats keeper Ryan Sully to secure a narrow 2-1 win and a place in the quarter-finals.

120

15 March 2009

Having taken the lead in the first minute of extra time, Celtic seal an Old Firm Scottish League Cup Final win with a second goal in the dying seconds. With Rangers desperately pushing forwards in search of an equaliser, Celtic work the ball out to Aiden McGeady on the left flank and he uses his pace to move past defender Kirk Broadfoot before cutting into the box, and as he is about to finish a fine individual goal, Broadfoot clips McGeady's leg to give the referee two simple decisions – one, to award an obvious penalty, and two, to show Broadfoot a straight red card for a clear professional foul. McGeady demands the ball, places it down and sends keeper Allan McGregor the wrong way to make it 2-0 and seal a 14th League Cup success.

Coin toss

26 November 1969

Celtic had just conceded the goal that meant the European Cup second-round second leg against Benfica – who had legendary striker Eusébio among their number – at the Estadio da Lu ended 3-3 on aggregate. The Portuguese had recovered from losing 3-0 at Parkhead to stage an amazing recovery. With no extra time or penalty shoot-out in place at the time, the standard way to settle a drawn tie was by the tossing of a coin.

Though the normal way was to get both captains into the centre circle to toss the coin, the referee instead took the captains – Celtic's Billy McNeill and Mário Coluna of Benfica – to his dressing room. The ref asked McNeill to call and he said 'heads' – and it was heads. The ref then informed McNeill the coin toss had been to decide which of the captains would spin the coin. The ref handed McNeill a silver Dutch two-guilder piece to toss into the air to determine which club progressed to the next round.

After asking his manager Jock Stein what to call and being told to make his own decision, McNeill stuck with his hunch to call heads and he flicked the coin high – it landed on the dressing-room floor, rolled to the ref's foot, and lay flat. It was heads. Celtic were through in the most bizarre manner possible and McNeill got to keep the coin as a souvenir. Just don't ask what minute all this happened in!

Penalty shoot-outs

It's the nail-biting finish many can't bear to watch – the dreaded penalty shoot-out to decide who wins what. Celtic have a decent record in penalty shoot-outs over the years – here are some of the most memorable ones ...

European Cup semi-final second leg: Celtic v Inter Milan

19 April 1972

Celtic and Inter Milan cannot be separated after two matches and extra time resulting in a penalty shoot-out at Hampden Park. With a crowd of more than 73,000 behind the Celts and playing on home soil (technically), could Jock Stein's side repeat the heroics of 1967's Lisbon Lions against Inter – this time at the semi-final stage of the European Cup?

Inter took the first spot-kick ...

- Facchetti (Inter Milan) – scores – 0-1
- Dixie Deans (Celtic) – misses – 0-1

- Frustalupi (Inter Milan) – scores – 0-2
- Jimmy Craig (Celtic) – scores – 1-2
- Pellizzaro (Inter Milan) – scores – 1-3
- Jinky Johnstone (Celtic) – scores – 2-3
- Jair (Inter Milan) – scores – 2-4
- Pat McCluskey (Celtic) – scores – 3-4
- Mazzola (Inter Milan) – scores – 3-5
- Bobby Murdoch (Celtic) – scores – 4-5

Inter Milan win 5-4 on penalties.

*Both teams had to take the full five penalties, even though Inter scored all five and Murdoch's penalty made no difference. The Italians went on to play Ajax in the final, losing 2-0.

29 August 2007

Celtic and Spartak Moscow battle for a place in the Champions League group stages but cannot be separated after two legs and extra time. Having drawn 1-1 in Moscow, Celtic again draw 1-1 at Parkhead meaning the scores are level and extra time is needed. Both sides missed a penalty in extra time meaning the game went to a penalty shoot-out ...

- Gary Caldwell (Celtic) – scores – 1-0
- Mozart (Spartak Moscow) – scores – 1-1
- Shinsuke Nakamura (Celtic) – misses – 1-1
- Yegor Titov (Spartak Moscow) – misses – 1-1
- Jan Vennegoor of Hesselink (Celtic) – scores – 2-1

- Roman Pavlyuchenko (Spartak Moscow) – scores – 2-2
- Derek Riordan (Celtic) – scores – 3-2
- Florin Șoavă (Spartak Moscow) – scores – 3-3
- Maciej Żurawski (Celtic) – scores – 4-3
- Maksym Kalynychenko (Spartak Moscow) – misses – 3-4

Celtic win 4-3 on penalties.

28 January 2009

Celtic and Dundee United could not be separated in the Scottish League Cup semi-final at Hampden Park, drawing 0-0 in normal time and it was still 0-0 after a further 30 minutes of extra time. An epic penalty shoot-out ensued ...

- Willo Flood (Dundee United) – scores – 1-0
- Scott McDonald (Celtic) – scores – 1-1
- Jon Daly (Dundee United) – scores – 2-1
- Gary Caldwell (Celtic) – scores – 2-2
- Warren Feeney (Dundee United) – scores – 3-2
- Shinsuke Nakamura (Celtic) – scores – 3-3
- Craig Conway (Dundee United) – scores – 4-3
- Barry Robson (Celtic) – scores – 4-4
- Paul Dixon (Dundee United) – scores – 5-4
- Georgios Samaras (Celtic) – scores – 5-5
- Morgaro Gomis (Dundee United) – scores – 6-5
- Lee Naylor (Celtic) – scores – 6-6

CELTIC MINUTE BY MINUTE

- Garry Kenneth (Dundee United) – scores – 7-6
- Marc Crosas (Celtic) – scores – 7-7
- David Robertson (Dundee United) – scores – 8-7
- Scott Brown (Celtic) – scores – 8-8
- Lee Wilkie (Dundee United) – misses – 8-8
- Glenn Loovens (Celtic) – misses – 8-8
- Mihael Kovačević (Dundee United) – scores – 9-8
- Andreas Hinkel (Celtic) – scores – 9-9
- Łukasz Załuska (Dundee United) – scores – 10-9
- Artur Boruc (Celtic) – scores – 10-10
- Willo Flood (Dundee United) – misses – 10-10
- Scott McDonald (Celtic) – scores – 10-11

Celtic win 11-10 on penalties.

Scottish Cup Final: Celtic v Hearts

20 December 2020

After a thrilling 3-3 draw with Hearts in the coronavirus-delayed 2019/20 Scottish Cup Final, Celtic and Hearts are forced to go all the way to a penalty shoot-out to decide the winners of the trophy – here's what happened ...

- Steven Naismith (Hearts) – scores – 0-1
- Leigh Griffiths (Celtic) – scores – 1-1
- Michael Smith (Hearts) – scores – 1-2
- Callum McGregor (Celtic) – scores – 2-2

- Oliver Lee (Hearts) – scores – 2-3
- Ryan Christie (Celtic) – misses – 2-3
- Stephen Kingsley (Hearts) – misses – 2-3
- Mikey Johnston (Celtic) – scores – 3-3
- Craig Wighton (Hearts) – misses – 3-3
- Kristoffer Ajer (Celtic) – scores – 4-3

Celtic win 4-3 on penalties and claim a quadruple treble in the process, as well as winning the Scottish Cup for the 40th time.